YOU CAN'T FOOL MOTHER NATURE

The Once and Future Triumph of Environmentalism

Byron Kennard

ISBN: 9798621831707
ISBN: 9781091219403

Published by
The Two Josephines Press
2220 20ᵗʰ Street, NW
Washington, DC 20009
bckennard@aol.com

Cover photo: Colourbox.com

Cover design: Joe Handy

Library of Congress Control Number: 2018675309

Printed on recycled paper
in the United States of America

Praise for Byron Kennard's

YOU CAN'T FOOL MOTHER NATURE

"Bold, upbeat, and witty — but behind the drollery, Kennard is shrewdly advocating the pursuit of radical ecological goals through conservative methods, signifying a sea change in thinking about the politics of the environment."

— **Peter H. Schuck**, Professor Emeritus, Yale Law School; Author, *One Nation Undecided: Clear Thinking About Five Hard Issues That Divide Us*

"Byron Kennard is one of the environmental movement's greatest organizers."

— **Amory Lovins**, Co-founder and Chief Scientist, Rocky Mountain Institute

"*In You Can't Fool Mother Nature*, Byron Kennard unveils a vision for the future to address the manifold threats our planet faces. He draws on his experience in the environmental movement to suggest the way forward on climate change and other challenges. In many instances, we know what needs to be done and how to do it. In others, we will need to draw on the innovative, entrepreneurial spirit of the coming generation. Kennard's writings should inspire this next generation to do what is necessary to preserve civilization, indeed life on earth as we know it."

— **Gordon Binder**, Chief of Staff, US Environmental Protection Agency, 1989-93

"Byron Kennard is that rare thing, a servant leader, a guide who helped many grassroots leaders around the USA speak out on multiple threats to our environment and human health. He was a key collaborator during my tenure as founding chair of Citizens for Clean Air in New York City in the late 1960s. I'm happy to affirm his role for so many of us activists!"

— **Hazel Henderson**, CEO, Ethical Markets Media; Author, *Mapping the Global Transition to the Solar Age*

"Byron Kennard is unique among social change activists in his expertise based on the real world of social change combined with his incredible knowledge of history.

His pioneering work in the environmental movement gave him a unique, practical knowledge of how social change really happens.

But it is his deep understanding of history that makes Byron's insights so insightful and helpful.

Today's social change leaders would benefit from Byron's practical insight combined with this deep understanding of history. It's this combination that makes this book so critical to anyone interested in social change for the better."

— **Rich Tafel,** Founder of The Public Squared, a public policy training program for nonprofits and social entrepreneurs; Author, *Party Crasher: A Gay Republican Challenges Politics as Usual,* and the founder of Log Cabin Republicans

"Community organizers often succeed
by declining to take credit for progress achieved
but, instead, attributing it to others. That's how — back
in the 1960s — Byron Kennard played a seminal role in
helping to create the modern environmental movement.
He did this not because he's modest (he's not), but
because he knew it would work. *And it did!*

What Kennard and other environmental pioneers
launched all those years ago has evolved into one of the
most powerful and constructive social movements
in world history.

Sixty years later — as catastrophic climate change
threatens the planet — Kennard, at age 82, takes stock
of the movement he helped create, concluding that it
remains our best hope for ensuring a secure future for
current and future generations."

-- **Peter Harnik**, "Global 500" Achiever,
Friends of the United Nations Environment Program; former
Coordinator, Environmental Action

"Having spent 25 years in early childhood education, I discovered how many of the boys and girls I have cared for loved exploring everything from dinosaurs to locusts.

One mother decorated her 4-year old daughter's birthday cake with insects because she loved insects so much. Anyone who has ever had small children knows of their innate love of the natural world when exposed to it.

And that's why, for me, Byron Kennard's *You Can't Fool Mother Nature* is so critical: we need a new understanding of how we are all part of the natural world, partners with all of life on earth, plants, animals, insects, and even the microbial world that we cannot see.

You Can't Fool Mother Nature outlines a course of action to engage young and old in ensuring that the natural world is secure and productive."

— **Michael Rawson**, retired pre-school teacher, MA Early Childhood Education

"Byron Kennard was an environmentalist even before there was an environmental movement. Starting in the 1960s, he has been a senior strategist and mentor to several generations of environmental leaders. I remember a day early in 1970 when a co-worker came back to the office, fired up with ideas Byron had given her. But it wasn't just the ideas, he gave us the courage to go out and do it.

— **George Alderson,** in 1970, became the first registered lobbyist for the environment. He went on to lead legislative campaigns for Friends of the Earth and for The Wilderness Society. He is the author of *How You Can Influence Congress.*

"**Kennard is one of the unheralded leaders of the modern environmental movement. This book offers fascinating insight into how the movement formed and, at long last, should award long overdue recognition of his extraordinary contribution to it.**"

—*W. Michael McCabe*, Executive Director of Earth Day '80, former Deputy Administrator, US Environmental Protection Agency

"Despite the dismal reality
of how we've beaten and robbed Mother Nature,
Byron Kennard's pithy and practical new book
leaves one with a revitalized sense of confidence
about the potential for nature's recovery despite
the counter-acting absurdities of human behavior.

A lot of wisdom is packed into each line of
thought he expresses, much of it derived
from the vital context of history.

Humanity will be lucky if its struggle to
continue here on earth into the next century is
guided by wisdom that Kennard imparts here."

— **Carl Sferrazza Anthony**, historian, author of works
on presidential families and spouses and a website on
American political culture

You Can't Fool Mother Nature

x

Dedicated to the memory of the late
Dr. E. F. Schumacher (1911-1977),
Author of *Small is Beautiful:
Economics as If People Mattered*

Fritz Schumacher was my friend,
colleague, and mentor.
He taught me — and the world — to
acknowledge and value
the primacy of scale
as a factor in all human endeavors.

Table of Contents

Introduction   1

1. Two Vows — Sixty Years Apart   8

2. Environmentalism's Past Triumph   16

3. Upgrading the Culture   23

4. The Futility of Politics   28

5. Environmentalism's Future Triumph   35

6. Back to Nature. . . documentaries   42

7. Facilitating the Inevitable   49

8. Everything Really is Connected to Everything Else   53

9. The Renaissance: Everything Old is New Again   59

10. Me & Martin Luther   63

11. Liberty, Equality, Diversity   68

12. Edmund Burke's Earth Day Speech   74

13. Creative Destruction is Good for the Environment   81

14. **The Irresistible Power of Self-Organizing Systems**   87

15. **Small Business: the Great Green Hope**   90

16. **Yes, Maggie Thatcher, There is Such a Thing as Society**   94

17. **Mother Nature's Politics: She's a Conservative + a Liberal**   99

18. **Mother Nature's Got a Hold on You**   107

19. **Rewilding: A Step Backwards into the Future**   112

20. **Conservatives ♥ Clean Energy**   122

21. **We Can Learn, We Can Change, We Can Grow**   130

Epilogue   136

About the Author   146

Acknowledgements   148

Appendix #1 **Honor Roll: My Green Pioneers**   159

Appendix #2 **The Environmental Justice Movement**   249

Index   255

Introduction

Lordy, lordy, lordy! The Sixties — the *fabled* Sixties — began *sixty years ago!* I can't believe it! Tell me it ain't so! *Sixty years!* That's longer than the lifespans of John Keats and Percy Shelley combined! But to me, it seems like *yesterday!* Well, at least it explains how I got to be an old man with one foot in the grave.

Forgive me, I've no right to complain. Back in the Sixties, when I was a young man and light on my feet, I had a whopping good time. It was an unparalleled era of social and political ferment, and I was in the thick of it, a young whippersnapper determined to make the world a better place. Now, that's a tall order in any era, I know. Saints have tried it and failed. But — guess what? — *I succeeded!*

I'm talking about the time in the Sixties when I worked as a community organizer, running around the country helping form local civic groups to combat air and water pollution. This local organizing paid off big time when Earth Day rolled around in 1970.

The environmental revolution inaugurated by Earth Day made the world *a much better place* — and in a million ways too, both large and small.

Some ways in which the environmental revolution changed the world for the better

•   *The Environmental Protection Agency (EPA) banned DDT (1972), a pesticide that was spreading rapidly through the food chain and damaging entire ecosystems; DDT almost made the bald eagle extinct. The ban paved the way for reducing or eliminating other toxic chemicals, like PCBs.*

•   *Access to safe drinking water was made a legal right by the Safe Drinking Water Act (1974), which established national standards for acceptable levels of pollutants in water.*

•   *Under provisions of the Clean Air Act, emission reductions and efficiency rules for automobiles were imposed for the first time (1975). As a result, lead levels in the air have been dramatically reduced.*

•   *Plants were added to Endangered Species list for the first time (1978). Initially the list was made up only of threatened animals. Examples of plants now protected are orchids, cacti, pitcher plants, some cycads and palms, ginseng, goldenseal, and some tropical timber trees.*

•   *The 1987 Montreal Protocol led to a significant reduction of CFCs, which were depleting the earth's ozone layer, and points the way to an international response to escalating levels of greenhouse gases that are fueling climate change.*

•   *The EPA Superfund program was created in 1980 to clean up toxic sites where, for decades, chemical and plastic manufacturers had dumped tons of dangerous pollutants. As of June 2019, 413 such sites have been cleaned up. Along with other programs, Superfund underscored the importance of the environmental justice movement.*

•   Giant strides have been made in preserving nature in national parks, wilderness areas, wild and scenic rivers, along with historic sites. In this regard, 1984 was a banner year. A total of 8.6 million acres were then designated as areas protected by the Wilderness Act. These areas were located in 21 states, including Arizona, California, Florida, New Mexico, and Wyoming.

•   The Ocean Dumping Ban Act (1988) made it illegal to dump municipal sewage sludge and industrial waste in the ocean. Until then, the government had no control over ships intentionally dumping medical waste, garbage, chemicals, radioactive agents, and other harmful substances into the ocean.

•   The Land and Water Conservation Fund has helped finance over 42,000 parks and recreation areas across the country. Along with protecting wilderness and wildlife, the fund helps to preserve working forests and ranchlands, backcountry trails, ball fields, battlefields, and other historic and cultural sites.

For a fuller account, see "Environmentalism's Past Triumph" which follows on page sixteen.

Now, I didn't pull off the environmental revolution all by myself, of course. That's not the way grassroots social movements succeed. Certainly, I played my part, but so did many others, some of whom I knew and worked with, but many of whom I did not. I could *not* know them all, not even if I networked my ass off for a hundred years.

Here's the key: *the environmental revolution was the result of countless uncoordinated acts by countless uncoordinated actors.* In my experience, if the world is actually going to be changed for the better, *this* is the best way to do it. It's *social*, not *political*. And it smacks of undeniable authenticity.

In this connection, I'm thinking of my esteemed colleague, Brock Evans. Brock is a legendary figure in the environmental movement, a leader in achieving protection of the North Cascades National Park, Hells Canyon, the Boundary Waters Wilderness, and many other natural areas around the country. Brock, who's still kicking (and writing his memoirs), is now President of the Endangered Species Coalition.

It so happens that Brock and I belong to a mutual admiration society. Oh, how I wish you could hear the nice things Brock says about me! Well, actually, you *can*. By artful pre-arrangement, I've solicited this statement from him, which I find handy for quoting:

"Back in the 1960s, I was one of the grassroots organizers working alongside Byron Kennard and other green pioneers to create a new consciousness about the urgent need to protect the environment. We succeeded — and in spades too! Ultimately, the seeds we planted grew into one of the great social and political movements in history, winning the adherence of millions of people the world over. This grand accomplishment demonstrates the power of grassroots ferment to change *history* — and for *the better* too! What a tale!

"In his new book, *You Can't Fool Mother Nature*, Byron describes how this political magic happened, drawing on his intimate familiarity with organic political change, a process in which top-down, centralized leadership is neither needed nor wanted.

"As Byron tells the story, organic political change consists of a plethora of self-organizing, small-scale, and decentralized actions by countless concerned citizens. Now, today, as climate change overtakes us, Byron shows how this incomparably powerful tool can be mobilized on new fronts to combat the threat confronting us."

New fronts?! Hey, Brock, old pal, you've hit the nail on the head! Some people might wonder why I've written a book that dredges up all this old stuff from sixty years ago —*especially* when we're being overtaken by catastrophic climate change — *especially* when the time we've got to combat this unparalleled threat may be running out.

What we did before, we must do again — and damned quick too. Thank heaven, I say, for the environmental revolution! We've learned so much in the past 50 years! We are not defenseless! We are not doomed! I feel like climbing up on the roof and shouting out loud: *"Hey, everybody! Listen! We know what to do, and we know how to do it! That's half the battle!*

- We know how to green roofs; we know how to green buildings; we know how to green neighborhoods; we know how to green communities; we know how to green *everything under the sun*! Let's do it!

- We've learned that rewilding vast portions of the Earth may be the most direct, practical, economic, and efficient way we have to combat climate change. That's because Mother Nature does almost all the work, and she works for *free,* and she works *fast*. Let's let her do it!

In our present predicament, this legacy of social and political learning is precious stuff. I intensely desire to transmit this legacy to young climate activists like Greta Thunberg who are, I think, calling for it. Ponder this quote from her: "All political movements in their present form have failed, but homo sapiens have not yet failed. Yes, we are failing, but there is still time to turn everything around. We can still fix this."

In this connection, I'm thinking of Catherine Lerza's views on this subject. Back in the old days, Cathy was a one-woman social change whirlwind. She edited *Environmental Action* magazine and the book, *Food for People, Not for Profit*. She co-founded and directed the National Family Farm Coalition and also served as associate director of the Rural Coalition.

Forgive my boasting, but Cathy also has a lot of nice things to say about me. Once again, by artful prearrangement:

"Byron has always known that saving the planet requires people, organized people, who won't take no for answer. More than 50 years ago, his commitment to organizing people on behalf of the planet came to glorious fruition as Earth Day 1970.

'Today, as young people around the world take to the streets, the ballot box, and the halls of political power to stop climate change, Byron is once again on the scene when we need him most.

"This time it's his book, *You Can't Fool Mother Nature,* a distillation of experience and political savvy, that arrives just in time. Not just because the 50th anniversary of Earth Day is around the corner, but because the next generation will find in its beautifully written pages a history lesson or two (or three), smart political strategy, pathways to real change, and a lot of inspiration."

Thanks, Cathy, for laying it on so thick (and I didn't even have to twist your arm).

Now, let's move on to the main course.

But first there's something I want you to know: to pull off this book, I've ransacked tons of old files and articles that I've published over the years, mostly on *GreenBiz* and the *Huffington Post*. So, it's a grab-bag, a collection of essays, not an integrated whole.

Some of these essays are brand spanking new, written especially for this book. I'm hoping and praying that this mishmash collection *adds up to more than the sum of its parts*. Wouldn't it be dandy if something magical like that happened *on its own*? Frankly, I could use the help. I'm grappling here with multiple threats to the survival of civilization, and maybe even, to the human race. That's a lot to handle, and I'm not getting any younger.

1

Two Vows — Sixty Years Apart

I got the idea for this book one night in 2018 when I was watching a BBC nature documentary on television. It was one of those extraordinarily beguiling programs presented by Sir David Attenborough (whom I hereby nominate for the position of Honorary President of the Planet).

Specifically, I was watching the first episode of *Blue Planet II*, titled *One Ocean*. Oh, boy, what a show! It's full of rare and unusual shots of ocean wildlife, from the tiniest baby turtles to the largest sharks. I was blown away — but then I often am by the nature documentaries produced in recent years by BBC, PBS *Nature*, *National Geographic*, and others. They garner universal praise, they astonish and overawe viewers, and they consistently win accolades from critics.

(Sebastian Smee, the *Washington Post's* Pulitzer Prize-winning art critic, believes that, "Nature films are the greatest art of our time.")

Wonders <u>never</u> seen before —

Blue Planet II — in wave after wave of exquisite photography — displays footage of natural wonders we've never seen before. We see, for example, footage of Yeti crabs, a species first discovered in 2006 off the coast of Easter Island. Yeti Crabs grow large colonies of bacteria on their hairy claws, letting it flourish there before "farming" it and slurping it up. "Yeti crabs grow their own food," says Sir David.

The tuskfish is another wonder to behold. It's a marine fish with strong teeth that lives in the Indian Ocean. It uses its teeth to pick up clamshells, which it then beats against massive coral reefs until the shell breaks open, so the fish can eat the meat inside. "Here is a fish that uses tools," says Sir David.

Here's still another wonder. The giant trevally, a species of large marine fish native to the Indian and Pacific Oceans, can leap out of the water to catch seabirds that fly too close to the ocean's surface (often fledgling terns, out testing their wings). Says Sir David: "Here's a fish that, amazingly, has a brain capable of calculating the air speed, altitude, and trajectory of a bird."

Wonders <u>seen</u> as never before —

If viewing these fabulous animals for the first time isn't totally mind-blowing, here's what is: *viewing them almost as if we were the animals themselves.*

Thanks to the latest technology innovation in filmmaking, we can practically do that. The wonders we behold on screen are brought to life with the help of cutting-edge technology, such as 4K cameras, remote recording, and aerial drones with cameras. Oh, how the wonders pile up!

In BBC's *Planet Earth II* series, for example, we visit chipmunks in their den. We watch chimpanzees using tools to crack nuts. We follow alongside the beautiful indri (a large, short-tailed lemur) as she strides through the forest in

Madagascar. We watch grizzly bears scratching their backs on trees, like pole dancers.

The standout is probably *Nature: Animals with Cameras,* a PBS production. Here animals, as they go about their business, wear custom-built cameras attached to their bodies. These cameras go where human camera operators can't go, and camera-wearing animals film their own stories. In the Kalahari Desert, the producers put cameras on Meerkats. In Cameroon, they fitted cameras to chimpanzees. In Argentina, they fitted tiny cameras to penguins.

Here's how PBS (accurately) describes the show:

"Astonishing collar-camera footage reveals newborn Kalahari Meerkats below ground for the first time, unveils the hunting skills of Magellanic penguins in Argentina, and follows the treetop progress of an orphaned chimpanzee in Cameroon . . . viewers will sprint across the savannah with a cheetah, plunge into the ocean with a seal, and swing through the trees with a chimp!"

Watch it and weep —

I'm an 82-year-old man who seldom weeps, but I sometimes weep watching these magnificent nature documentaries. I weep in awe of the beauty and wonder of nature. It makes me glad to be alive, glad to possess the capacity to perceive and appreciate such beauty and wonder. It makes me feel *connected* to the universe.

But I also weep in despair. These nature documentaries reveal — as they *ought* to, as they *must* — the deadly peril this beauty faces from humanity's assault on natural systems.

To me, the contrast between the beauty, on the one hand, and the threat to the beauty, on the other, is almost unbearable. Within me, I feel a grim determination forming. *On the spot, I vow to do whatever I can to halt the further destruction of nature.*

Flashback!

One night in June 1962, I was in bed reading the *New Yorker* when I ran across an article excerpted from a forthcoming book by a marine biologist named Rachel Carson. The book, titled *Silent Spring*, was a critique of chlorinated hydrocarbon pesticides and the immense environmental damage caused by their use. (*Silent Spring* first appeared in three serialized excerpts in the *New Yorker*. It wouldn't be published in book form until September 1962.)

Carson's critique was passionate and persuasive. Here's an example:

"The control of nature is a phrase conceived in arrogance, born of the Neanderthal age of biology and philosophy when it was supposed that nature exists for the convenience of man. The concepts and practices of applied entomology for the most part date from that Stone Age of science. It is our alarming misfortune that so primitive a science has armed itself with the most modem and terrible weapons and that in turning them against the insects it has also turned them against the earth."

Reading *Silent Spring,* I was overcome by powerful emotions. (Did I cry? Maybe. I can't remember. It was a long time ago.) I do know that, on the spot, I *vowed* to do whatever I could, as an individual, to fight the pollution of the environment. I took the job on. At that precise moment, I became an environmentalist.

As noted, that moment of commitment occurred almost sixty years ago; and today, I'm still laboring away at fulfilling it, even in my decrepitude. Now, I must ask: did I make any difference?

So far, (as you know all too well) I've been congratulating myself for making the world a better place. Maybe I ought to keep my mouth shut.

I hate to say it, but the environment is worse off now than it was when I first vowed to make a difference. Almost 50 years after Earth Day, deforestation is proceeding at a fast clip, especially in the Amazon rainforest, "the lungs of the planet." Freshwater tables across the globe, including parts of America, are falling precipitously. The world's oceans are deteriorating rapidly as billions of pounds of trash, plastic, and other pollutants are dumped into them each year. Well over half of the world's major fisheries are severely depleted or overfished.

More and more animal and plant species are endangered, not fewer. These threats are largely the result of human activity. Honeybees, for example, are going extinct because of excessive use of pesticides in crops. Given the vital pollinating role bees play in agricultural production, the extinction of bees might well lead to worldwide famine.

I've saved the worst for last. The news reports that the journal *BioScience* just published a statement declaring that the world's people face "untold suffering due to the climate crisis" unless there are major transformations to global society. That's scary enough, but here's what's even scarier: this warning comes from more than 11,000 scientists from 153 nations.

"We declare clearly and unequivocally that planet Earth is facing a climate emergency," the statement says. "To secure a sustainable future, we must change how we live. This entails major transformations in the ways our global society functions and interacts with natural ecosystems."

The changes urged by the scientists include ending population growth, leaving fossil fuels in the ground, halting forest destruction, and slashing meat eating.

According to the scientists, there is no time to lose. "The climate crisis has arrived and is accelerating faster than most scientists expected. It is more severe than anticipated, threatening natural ecosystems and the fate of humanity."

(Do you mind if I take this *personally*?! Just for a moment, anyway? Just long enough to spew some venom? It looks to me like *somebody* screwed up along the way — and really *bad* too! Well, it wasn't *me,* for chrissakes! And not my fellow green pioneers either! We've been agitating about this crap for over half a century?! Did I spend all those years spitting into the wind? Frankly, sometimes I'm glad I'm an old man with one foot in the grave. With any luck, I'll be dead and gone when the shit hits the fan. End of rant.)

Post-rant Reflection

After much agonizing introspection, here's where I come out: what we've got here is a nip-and-tuck situation. But nip-and-tuck means that the outcome is in doubt — too close to call — which means, at least, *we've got a chance.* So, let's grab it. And we are not defenseless! I repeat, thanks to the environmental revolution, *we know what to do, and we know how to do it.* That's half the battle.

*In the 50 years
since Earth Day
over half of new electricity
coming onto the global grid
and into buildings is renewable energy.*

*Variable wind and solar
along with vastly improved
storage of renewable energy
now significantly undercuts
the natural gas generation business.*

*And in recent decades,
energy efficient lighting
and electric heat pumps
have reduced global electricity use by 20%.*

*Now the planet is on the verge of creating
self-healing grids in energy, as we have in
communications and in the world wide web.*

*Hang onto your hats!
The environmental revolution
is still on the march!"*

— **Scott Sklar**, *former Political Director
The Solar Lobby;
former Executive Director
Solar Energy Industries Association;
Adjunct Professor, The George Washington University*

2

Environmentalism's Past Triumph

***How Social Institutions Were Transformed by the
Environmental Revolution***

Okay, let's revisit the proposition discussed earlier that —
thanks to the environmental revolution and its manifold
beneficial consequences — *we know what to do, and we know
how to do it*. This proposition permeates the social analysis
presented in this book. In fact, I argue that the environmental
revolution triumphed in nearly every sector of society.

In the half-century that's passed since Earth Day, the many
changes wrought by the environmental revolution have
endured; they've progressed; some have flourished. But — with
the passage of time — they've been taken for granted and so are
overlooked or discounted. *No more!* Now, we must trot them out
anew, celebrate them once again, and — to be blunt about it —
ride them for all they're worth.

Let's take a brief tour of social history since Earth Day, and
I'll show you a batch of environmentalism's past achievements,
building blocks we can use to mount a defense against
catastrophic climate change.

The entire educational system has been greened, from top to bottom, from grade school to grad school.

The radical and profound consequences of the environmental revolution penetrated all sectors of society, but none more so than the field of education, where a new discipline quickly emerged.

Environmental education, obviously, is about teaching school kids about ecology, the functioning of natural systems, and the need for conservation and protection of the environment. But it also involves the job of enabling professional educators to train and equip others to become professional environmental educators.

This is a new of form of education that is — and *has* to be — extraordinarily broad-based, involving aspects of science, technology, geography, engineering, and economics, not to mention politics, history, cultural and social studies, the arts, and many other disciplines. Environmental education covers, as it should, everything under the sun.

Today, environmental education takes place everywhere under the sun, not only in formal classrooms but outdoors in nature centers, parks and wilderness areas, and in art and science museums.

Especially significant here is the worldwide effort *to actually green* schools and campuses. This is a big deal. According to *The Princeton Review Guide to Green Colleges*, around the world a total of 413 colleges and university campuses are actively working to make themselves carbon neutral.

On green campuses, students investigate their school's site, energy use, water use, and its waste and recycling practices. The aim is to make the campus a "living lab" that provides hands-on opportunities for experiential learning by students.

Campus gardens, for example, are becoming a growing trend at colleges and universities. In addition to reducing emissions caused by food transportation, students also get the opportunity to learn about urban gardens, organic agriculture, and sustainable food systems.

The Professions

The ideas associated with the environmental revolution have permeated every form of intellectual endeavor engaged in by humans and has produced a raft of new professions. Just ponder this list:

- Environmental Economics
- Environmental Education
- Environmental Engineering
- Environmental Health & Medicine
- Environmental Law
- Environmental Media
- Environmental Planning & Design
- Environmental Science & Technology

Green Businesses and Industries

Look too at all the other *new businesses and industries* that were spawned by the Environmental Revolution: organic agriculture, renewable energy, energy efficiency, distributed energy, alternative transportation, eco-tourism, recycling, and pollution control. And, in every instance, these green businesses and industries are growing at a faster pace than their conventional counterparts.

All in all, environmental protection is now a major industry, generating hundreds of *billions of dollars a year in sales.*

Green Jobs

Combine the impact of all these new green businesses and industries with the impact of new clean technologies and the result is the creation of millions of *new clean jobs* — far, far more in number than the dirty jobs destroyed when polluting industries go under.

Green Entrepreneurship

All over the world, countless *tinkerers and entrepreneurs* have taken up the environmental cause. They're at work fashioning innovative technologies to meet our material needs without harming natural systems. Many are now working to develop advanced battery storage systems for renewable energy. When this technology hits the market, the fossil fuel boys will be in the fight of their lives.

Upstart "green" small entrepreneurial businesses are now at work in practically every country. They are producing technological innovations that make solar power cheaper than coal, that make lighting systems and automobile engines vastly more efficient, and that make possible the storage of huge amounts of renewable energy at low cost.

Green Small Business

All over the world, countless *small business people* are at work greening themselves to meet the new consumer demand for green this and organic that.

For example, today when a new grocery is opened, it's amply stocked with organic produce. When a new restaurant, bakery, or delicatessen opens up, the owner loudly proclaims that it uses ingredients that are fresh and locally produced. This is good business. Today that's what consumers want to hear.

Leading the Way: States, Regions, and Cities

Though anti-environmentalists have subverted the political system at the Federal level, they've failed to subvert the entire system, which is, thank heaven, decentralized. Thus, many *States, regions, and localities* are vigorously tackling climate change, aiming to achieve zero-carbon buildings, 100 percent clean transportation, 100 percent renewable electricity, and zero waste.

Seventeen states have declared their intent to get 50 percent of their electricity from clean energy sources by 2025. Eighty-one American cities have adopted a 100 percent renewable energy goal. Many have promised that all new buildings in their jurisdictions will produce net zero carbon by 2030.

This is solid groundwork; and, if it's expanded in the next few years, we might well be grappling with climate change in a serious and effective way.

Greening Big Business

Finally, let's acknowledge that many *big businesses* are greening too. Corporate leaders are not dopes when it comes to climate change. They can see which way the wind is blowing.

The good news here is that hundreds of major corporations located all over the world have now pledged to adopt science-based emissions reduction targets, many pledging to being fully renewable. This isn't because governments have mandated it. It's because renewable energy is cost competitive and profitable for companies to use.

Many of the biggest companies making renewable energy commitments are now asking their suppliers to become 100 percent renewable too. Among them are Apple and Ikea.

Hey, we've covered half the world

That's impressive, right? How many movements conquer half the world? But — impressive as it sounds — there's another half the world I haven't even mentioned yet. And many super-smart people will argue passionately that *it's the most important half*.

Okay, well then, let's keep moving. Let's go survey the culture.

*Politically, it seems like half the world
has gone off the deep end;
and the large extent to which this mass irrationality
is anti-science, anti-intellectual, anti-environmental
and — alas! — even anti-nature baffles me.*

*Okay, so right-wing nuts despise fags, kikes, spics, feminazis,
and uppity blacks (their terms, not mine)
— they've made that obscenely obvious — but what on earth
have they got against dear old Mother Nature?*

*There's got to be something.
Nowadays much of the world's population — maybe a third
or even more — is actively embracing what might be called
anti-environmentalism.*

*Politicians succeed by telling people what they want to hear.
A lot of people don't want to be told the climate change is for real
and that humans are the cause of it.
They'd rather bury their heads in the sand.
So, demagogic anti-environmental politicians have had a heyday
peddling climate denial.*

*Mother Nature, however,
tells people what they don't want to hear
— and she makes it stick. That's unforgivable.*

*Hey, maybe that's why anti-environmentalists
hate Mother Nature.* — The Author

3

Upgrading the Culture

If the struggle over environmental protection is viewed as a culture war, then it's clear that environmentalists have won hands down. This is nothing to sneeze at! Culture packs more actual clout in society than politics.

The Arts & Humanities

Let's start with the arts. Art has power that politics lacks. It can move, astonish, and rouse us in ways that politics cannot. Really powerful art can change society for the better. *Sometimes a single image alone can do it.*

Probably everyone alive has seen the famous 1972 photograph of Earth taken from space by the Apollo 17 astronauts. What power it exerts! Seeing our planet as a finite ball floating alone in the vast ocean of space *probably did more to establish a collective worldwide environmental consciousness than any other thing.* The sight of this image thrills me still, forty-six years after I first saw it.

I'm wondering, what image do anti-environmentalists have to display that makes their point? The almighty dollar sign?!

The arts and humanities hvave dedicated themselves to the cause of environmental protection. What an ally! In actions that combine both creativity and activism, painters, sculptors, writers, photographers, and others have made environmental protection a *cultural* priority.

Just for openers, ponder this: the Environmental Revolution was ignited by a *book*, Rachel Carson's *Silent Spring* published in 1963.

Millions of people who read *Silent Spring* were inspired to become environmentalists. I was one of them. Another was Ted Hughes, one of the twentieth century's greatest English poets. Hughes served as Poet Laureate of the United Kingdom from 1984 until his death in 1998.

Hughes is celebrated for his nature poetry, especially his poems about endangered species and wildlife extinction, including *Crow* (1971), *Cave Birds* (1979), *Flowers and Insects* (1986), and *Wolfwatching* (1990). But Hughes was also a dedicated environmental activist who lobbied politicians like Margaret Thatcher. The great poet attributed his political activism to having read *Silent Spring*. It all comes together.

Eco-fiction (ecologically oriented novels and prose) emerged in the 1970s after Earth Day, creating a new literary category that connects humanities and nature. Today eco-fiction addresses human-caused climate change — much of it focused on post-apocalyptic disasters.

Environmentalism also frequently serves as the theme in novels of such celebrated writers as Barbara Kingsolver, Cormac McCarthy, Edward Abbey, J.G. Ballard, Margaret Atwood, Peter Matthiessen, T.C. Boyle, and Wallace Stegner.

Take a look at what *museums* have done. Museums are among the most powerful drivers of education and social change in the world. They command an immense audience. In America alone, there are over 30,000 museums, where each year there are something like 850 million visits, 90 million by schoolchildren.

Museums are among the *greenest* institutions in the world. Ever since Earth Day, art, science, and natural history museums have staged countless exhibits and programs devoted to the environment and its protection. In recent decades, museums have sounded the alarm on global warming, staging hundreds of exhibits that explain the causes and effects of climate change.

Has there been a single museum exhibit anywhere in the world dedicated to the propagation of anti-environmentalism? I doubt it.

Pop Culture

The world of culture, of course, embraces *pop culture,* which is about as green as a culture can get. This too is nothing to sneeze at. Many social critics believe that pop culture is now *more influential* in American society than politics. (Ponder this: when all the doors to politics were slammed in their faces, gay same-sex marriage advocates called on the power of pop culture to transform public opinion in their favor. They pleaded their case through television sit-coms — and it worked!)

What's more powerful than *pop music?* Here I submit for your consideration Marvin Gaye's *Mercy Mercy Me,* Michael Jackson's *The Earth Song,* Joni Mitchell's *Big Yellow Taxi* ("They paved paradise to put up a parking lot"), and (*Nothing But*)

Flowers by Talking Heads. And, of course, I could list dozens, or even hundreds, of other green pop songs.

The *movies* too are suffused with environmentalism. After Earth Day, Hollywood made environmental issues a frequent subject of movies. Here are some personal favorites: *Chinatown, Soylent Green, The China Syndrome,* and *Silkwood.* All great motion pictures and great green propaganda!

Television, of course, is replete with environmental programing, including the great documentary series, *Nature*, on PBS. The Science Channel, The Discovery Channel, and the Sundance Channel also do really great stuff.

If, however, I had to choose only one example, it would be *The Simpsons,* the longest-running sitcom in television history and undoubtably one of the best shows ever. The environmental connection? You'll recall that the evil billionaire, Montgomery Burns, owns the nuclear power plant that's located in Springfield. It's where Homer Simpson works. Over the years, core meltdowns at the plant and the plant's pollution have served as plot devices for many episodes in the series.

In passing, I wonder how many hit songs, or movies, or TV shows have sold the public on climate denial? Just asking . . .

Tour ends here

This completes our tour of society and of the grand and glorious accomplishments of the environmental revolution. I trust you are suitably impressed. Perhaps you are thinking: "Wow, with all this going for us how can we miss? Combatting climate change ought to be a piece of cake!"

Well — take my advice, and don't jump to any conclusions. Not yet. Now collect your things and follow me.

A new tour starts here. We're going to explode the relationship of environmentalism to politics.

Fasten your seat belts! It's going to be a bumpy ride.

4

The Futility of Politics

How Environmental Politics Wound up in a Dead End

Let's go back to Square One. On April 22, 1970, twenty million people turned out across the country to demand protection of the environment, nearly ten percent of the US population at that time. Indeed, Earth Day was — and remains — the largest single *political* demonstration in American history. What did it achieve *politically*?

Earth Day kicked off a period of remarkable political success that was achieved in a remarkably *bipartisan* way. Indeed, viewed from the perspective of today's political gridlock, the overwhelming bipartisan support for environmental protection in the early days seems unimaginable. Well, rub your eyes in amazement, it actually happened.

On the morning after Earth Day, we organizers woke to discover that overnight our new movement had acquired enormous political power. The phone was ringing off the hook with calls from members of Congress wanting to know how they could help — and these calls came from *both sides* of the aisle.

Ponder this: In 1970, the Clean Air Act passed Congress by votes of 73-0 in the Senate and 375-1 in the House. In 1972, the Clean Water Act passed the Senate 86-0 and the House 380-14. Can you imagine anything like this happening today?

And how's this for bipartisanship: the Republican President, "Tricky Dick" Nixon, behaving like a tree-hugging environmental activist? Well, he wasn't, of course. But he was a canny politician who could sense which way the wind power was blowing.

Look at his record as President. Starting in 1970, he issued an executive order creating the Environmental Protection Agency. Following that, he supported passage of the National Environmental Policy Act, the Clean Air Act, the Clean Water Act, and Endangered Species Act. All were enacted by Congress and signed into law by Nixon. (One glaring exception: President Nixon vetoed the 1972 Clean Water Act and never signed the legislation. It became law only after they overrode the President's veto, with strong bipartisan support.)

President Nixon did pretty well in the green rhetoric department as well. In his first State of the Union Address, he declared that:

"Restoring nature to its natural state is a cause beyond party and beyond factions. It has become a common cause of all the people of this country. It is a cause of particular concern to young Americans, because they more than we will reap the grim consequences of our failure to act on programs which are needed now if we are to prevent disaster later."

Oh, Tricky Dick, how I miss you and those halcyon days! "Disaster later" is making itself felt now. That's because — tragically — all this splendid bipartisanship was to be eroded and then completely destroyed by reactionary politics.

Earth Day's great political success, achieved through bipartisanship, was not to last. But it sure was fun while it did. Really, the intriguing question is how we environmentalists got away with it in the first place.

After all, we were attacking the all-mighty industrial order — the politically and economic dominant social order. And the most dominant force within this social order was the fossil fuel industry, the single richest and most powerful industry in all history. It took them a while, but the fossil fuel boys eventually connived to mount a counter-revolution to Earth Day and everything it stood for. Bear in mind that, in a democracy, money is the single most powerful force.

This counter-revolution was to clobber me personally in 1980.

Earth Day '80

Denis Hayes, Earth Day's national coordinator in 1970 (in 1980, he was the Director of the Federal Solar Energy Research Institute) asked me to take on the job of organizing a commemoration of the tenth anniversary of Earth Day. I readily agreed to do it, working as a volunteer.

Oh, boy, it turned out to be the hardest job I ever had, paid or unpaid. Earth Day '80, as we dubbed it, was in total contrast to the wingding I experienced in 1970. This time around everything I touched turned into ... well, *not* gold.

Mike McCabe, Earth Day '80's Executive Director, and I, as National Chair, busted our tails to commemorate the 10th anniversary in a big way. But, unlike 1970, when the press was eating out of our hand, the press in 1980 had largely turned on us. The anti-environmental counter-revolution was in full swing then and spreading big lies like mad. We were assaulted constantly with accusations that the environmental movement had destroyed many jobs and seriously harmed the economy.

Of course, in the spring of 1980, there was no way we could know it, but something else was blowing in the political wind: the Reagan revolution. Later, in November, Ronald ("If you've seen one tree, you've seen them all.") Reagan won the Presidency in a landslide, and Republicans took control of the Senate.

The winds had shifted, and a storm of anti-environmentalism was forming.

(Incidentally, in 1980, Earth Day's founder, Senator Gaylord Nelson, lost his bid for reelection to the Senate.)

Where We Stand Today — 40 Years Later

Now, it's obvious that many American citizens, probably a clear majority, are deeply concerned about the adverse climate change that's now enveloping the planet. This is especially true of those who've already suffered from more severe and frequent cyclones, droughts, floods, heat waves, hurricanes, tornadoes, and wildfires. As you might imagine, this gets tiresome.

Climate change is also causing rising levels of depression, anxiety, and fear. People feel powerless in the face of its onslaught. Psychiatrists are now treating people for what they've labelled "environmental melancholia." Young people are especially affected. Many are losing hope for their future. There are even reports that this concern has led some young people to decide not to have children.

What on earth is to be done?!

Naturally, all these concerned and troubled people expect the nation's political system to vigorously combat this grave threat to our wellbeing and our future. After all, that's what the political system *is for*, is it not? That's why it was *created*, right? That's why we *pay through the nose for the damned thing*, wouldn't you say?

It grieves me to say so, but these good people are barking up the wrong tree. As things stand, they ain't got a prayer.

America's political system has not been, and is not likely to be, galvanized to combat climate change. The system has been hopelessly corrupted by a flood of money from fossil fuel interests — the largest, richest, and most powerful industry in the history of industrialism.

If that weren't bad enough, the system has become so paralyzed by political polarization that virtually nothing can be done. We're lucky when Congress finds the gumption to pass a resolution authorizing the Thanksgiving holiday.

No consensus, no climate action

The vigorous mobilization of the political system requires the support of *a strong bipartisan consensus*. And in American politics today, the prospect of a bipartisan consensus is as dead as the dodo (a real bird hunted to extinction by humans 300 years ago). Here's the quandary. So long as a third (or more) of the population persists in denying that climate change exists, it will be impossible to forge a sufficiently strong consensus.

In their dreams, climate change activists envision the formation of a fiercely determined national spirit like that which materialized after the Japanese attack on Pearl Harbor in 1941. But what if one-third of the nation *denied that the attack had happened*? What if they claimed it was a *hoax*? What if they threw themselves in violent opposition to the war effort? Not even a devious political genius like FDR could have finagled that situation.

Political polarization renders bipartisan action impossible

This polarization stems from ugly roots in the culture — racism, misogyny, and homophobia, to name just three. These biases are so ancient and deep-seated as to be ineradicable. We are stuck with them. All we can do is bury them under rocks and hope they stay there.

(In the post-World War II era, in the 1950s when I was a starry-eyed youth, I remember saying to myself, "Well, at least, anti-semitism has been eradicated.")

What fuels the present pandemic of polarization is a backlash to the social progress made in recent decades in promoting equal rights.

- Throughout the country, men feel they're losing power to women. And it's true! They are! And masses of men resent this furiously.

- Throughout the country, white people feel they're losing power to people of color. And it's true! They are! And masses of white people resent this furiously.

There is no magic wand that can be waved to ameliorate this fury. So, let's not get our hopes up, not even if Democrats win bullet-proof Congressional majorities in 2020. The pandemic that is political polarization will infect their well-intentioned efforts to make progress on climate or anything else impossible.

To be utterly frank about it, it is my conviction that — when it comes to political polarization — progressives don't have a clue about how to solve it. Nobody does! It's a wound we'll have to wait on *time* to heal (But do we *have* the time? *Yuck*!)

Of course, in the meantime, the worldwide assault on democracy and the rule of law by right-wing populists — manifest in the US by the Trump maladministration — poisons any remaining hopes that conventional politics will be of any use.

Okay, are you now looking for a bridge you can jump off?! Well, cut that crap out! We're due for another departure.

Perk up, here's what I'm going to show you next: environmentalism is headed for a *future* triumph that's going to be even bigger than its past triumph. And we're going to pull it off by *evading* conventional politics and all its hang-ups and dead ends. We're doing to do it by playing *politics by other means.*

"The best leader is he,
who when his work is done,
the people look about and say,
'See what happened naturally.'"

-- Chinese proverb

5

Environmentalism's Future Triumph

If politics — *conventional* politics, politics *as usual* — is futile (or nearly so); if it leads to nothing but dead ends; if engaging with it is a waste of time and money that might be better spent elsewhere; and if — alas —the entire rotten game is counter-productive, then it makes sense to *disown* politics, to simply walk away from it.

Now, hang on, don't get your knickers in a twist! I'm not advocating *anarchy*. I'll explain. I don't want to disavow politics without recourse to a suitable alternative. There is one. It's called *politics by other means.*

Politics by other means works through cultural and social change, not through political change. It doesn't seek to win elections, set public policy, pass laws, or issue government regulations. It doesn't rely on command and control. Indeed, politics by other means evades and subverts politics as usual. It leapfrogs over politics as usual, tunnels beneath it, and runs rings around it.

Politics through other means is a lot more fun than politics as usual, which couldn't be more dreary and depressing. Politics by other means relies more on wit than wealth. Satire is its frequent weapon. It relies more on surprise than superior force.

Here's the icing on the cake. Politics by other means possesses the sublime pleasure of confounding the opposition, tying them in knots, and annoying the hell out of them. In the end, the poor bastards don't know what hit 'em.

Ponder this: when all the doors to politics were slammed in their faces, gay same-sex marriage advocates called on the power of pop culture to transform public opinion in their favor. They pleaded their case through *television sit-coms* — and it worked! Opponents of same sex marriage are still scratching their heads and wondering what the hell happened!

This phenomenon is nothing to sneeze at. Many social critics believe that pop culture is now *more influential* in American society than politics.

The same sex marriage victory vividly illustrates how the magic elixir of politics by other means actually works.

Politics by other means operates on the sly

Politics by other means hides in the shadows, donning obscurity like a protective cloak. Thereby it evades — and hoodwinks — a dangerously malfunctional political system. If politics by other means had a middle name it would be *stealth*.

Politics by other means operates through organic change, not through change that's planned or designed by central planners.

Organic change relies on small-scale, incremental changes over time not on across-the-board public policies with sweeping applications. Organic change consists of local efforts, not national. It operates from the bottom up, not from the top down.

Oh, the tactical advantages this brings! In the world of organic change, things are too small to see, too numerous to count, too diverse to classify, and too fast-moving to pin down.

Politics by other means relies on human ingenuity

Human beings are whizzes at devising new tools. It's what we do best. But, alas, we're not so hot at collaborating politically for the long-term common good. That's why politics by other means relies more on *new tools than new laws.*

Consider this: technology is often *more powerful* than law. No Congress ever mandated the invention of printing, electricity, the radio, the telephone, the automobile, the airplane, television, or the personal computer. Yet these technologies have changed society more than most laws could ever hope to do. This is why politics by other means relies on leadership by tinkerers and entrepreneurs, not by politicians and elected officials.

Politics by other means employs *creative destruction* in order to succeed. Creative destruction often occurs when obscure tinkerers and entrepreneurs devise radical innovations that take big established companies by surprise and render them vulnerable to disruption. If the big guys detect that a little guy is preparing to challenge their dominance, the big guys will ruthlessly deploy money and political clout to somehow derail the challenge.

Politics by other means relies on the power of self-organizing systems.

Look at how unfathomably complex natural systems — climate, oceans, and forests, for example — have evolved spontaneously to function in orderly fashion. Complex social systems also evolve spontaneously to function in orderly fashion.

I think this demands an example: giant industrial complexes do not evolve spontaneously. They are *planned*. The system that is the Fortune 500 is the product of a deliberate design by human beings. But the system of small business — like natural systems — is a miracle of self-organization. Look at small business as a system, and you'll see how closely it resembles the workings of nature. Small business and natural systems both are:

- Complex, interdependent webs that are totally decentralized;

- Ceasely dynamic, characterized by continuous cycles of birth, death, and rebirth;

- Flexible, adaptive, and constantly experimenting, grabbing any chance to plant new life, however slight, dim, or remote.

This is why I argue that small business is the best system we have for the restoration of natural systems.

Politics by other means relies on countless acts by countless actors to improve society

Organically, the best way to fundamentally improve society is through countless uncoordinated acts by countless uncoordinated actors. This flies in the face of convention.

Centralized authorities aim to better society through top-down, command and control mechanisms, but these efforts are often opposed by great masses of people who resent intrusions into their lives. It's better by far when social progress is achieved through *countless uncoordinated acts by countless uncoordinated actors.*

Where I come out . . .

Thank goodness, I say, that we have politics by other means to fall back on when the political system is corrupt, malfunctional, duplicitous, unresponsive, and unaccountable. I'm reminded of the joke about the old lady who adamantly refused to vote. "Vote? I never vote," she exclaimed. When asked why, she replied, "If you vote it only *encourages* the bastards!"

Thank goodness that consumers voting with their pocketbooks can compel business and industry to clean up their acts. This is one hell of a story.

In the years since Earth Day, a radical shift has occurred in the marketplace. Increasingly, consumers are basing purchasing decisions not just on value but on *their* values. Polls now indicate that *nine-in-10 consumers* expect companies to operate responsibly to embrace social and environmental concerns. This expectation is very broad. It includes how products are sourced, manufactured, packaged, and disposed of. It also includes such social aspects as how factory and farm workers are treated. And animals too! Pre-Earth Day, concern for such values scarcely entered into the conduct of business and industry.

And things keep getting greener and greener . . .

Today's Generation Z consists of young people who don't want to work for a big business, or own a car, or live in a single-family home on a large lot in a far-flung suburb. If this ain't a social revolution, I don't know what is. And I haven't even mentioned *meat-eating*.

WHERE'S THE BEEF?

Today something like 70 percent of the world population is either reducing meat consumption or leaving meat off the table altogether.

Climate scientists who are calling for urgent action to combat climate change list reduced consumption of meat as a top priority goal. In this, millennials are leading the way. They are eating much less meat. Over 25 percent of them are vegetarian or vegan. One-in-three millennial meals are meat-free.

Why? Many for reasons of personal health or economy. Many out of concern for animal welfare. And many because reducing meat consumption is one of the best ways to combat climate change.

Astounding but true: animal agriculture produces from 20 percent to 50 percent of all man-made greenhouse gas emissions. A global switch to diets that rely far less on meat and far more on vegetables, fruits, and other plant foods could reduce these food-related greenhouse gas emissions by two-thirds. Imagine that! Two-thirds! And all achievable though voluntary action, not through state coercion.

How many new laws would it take to secure such a big reduction? And what would these laws do? Would they prohibit meat consumption, like we did alcohol in the days of Prohibition? Back then police would raid speakeasies and arrest people caught drinking alcohol. Holy cow, can you imagine police raiding restaurants and arresting people eating steaks?

Isn't it much better that this massive reduction in meat consumption is achieved non-politically through mass consumer demand?

6

Back to Nature. . . documentaries

Great Art is Great Propaganda

I opened the discussion of this book describing how watching nature documentaries on television fortified my militant personal commitment to prevent the further destruction of nature. Here I close the discussion by describing a strategy that might inspire *other* people — *many* other people — to gird their loins too.

Please bear in mind my earlier observation that the best way to change society for the better is through countless acts by countless actors. That's the stew I'm hoping to stir up here: an implacable determination by masses of people to halt the abuse and exploitation of nature. That's the ticket!

I'll start by quoting once again Sebastian Smee's declaration that, "Nature films are the greatest art of our time." Great art can be wielded as a great propaganda tool. This idea is not original with me. Egyptian pharaohs discovered this, ages ago. The Roman Catholic Church has been doing it for tens of centuries. How might this tool be used to weaponize the powerful art that nature documentaries exert?

Let's start with Thoreau's belief that, "there is a subtle magnetism in Nature, which, if we unconsciously yield to it, will direct us aright." Let's make the most of this.

Abraham H. Maslow, the famous American psychologist, might be invoked here. He created *Maslow's hierarchy of needs,* a theory of psychological health predicated on fulfilling innate human needs in priority, culminating in self-actualization. In his book, *Religions, Values, and Peak-Experiences,* Maslow described nature as a catalyst for *peak experiences,* when humans experience deep joy and transcendental connectedness.

Connectedness! Ah, there's a word to conjure with! And, boy, do I ever! This sense of connectedness binds us to other people, to other life forms, to planetary ecology, and of course, ultimately to God. What force it has! So, I argue, connectedness is strong enough to overcome *tribalism.* It's strong enough to counter *political polarization.* (Beware, Donald Trump! Mother Nature is out gunning for you!)

When people personally experience nature's beauty and wonder they can be transformed and made better.

- I believe that human beings who directly connect with nature become healthier, wiser, and more compassionate.

- I believe that these humans are enveloped in a sense of *community* — a sense of being part of a magnificent whole.

- Finally, I believe that virtually every human being who lives and breathes is subject to this transformative power of nature *if they are exposed to it.*

But, clearly, they are not. Today, on average, Americans spend 87 percent of their time inside buildings. They spend 6 percent of their time in enclosed vehicles. Add it up. Americans spend a total of *93 percent* of their lives shut off from the out-of-doors. And what are they *doing* all this time? They're staring at screens on television sets, on computers, and on tablets and smartphones. On average, Americans are spending 11 hours per day *looking at pictures!*

Oh, dear, all this constant staring at screens seems lamentable, doesn't it? *Unhealthy, even.* How much better off people would be if they were outside in the fresh air, personally enjoying nature's extraordinary beauty.

Think of it! How wonderful it would be if everyone could be climbing mountains, hiking in forests, exploring jungles, sailing up the Amazon or down the Nile, or traveling on safari in East Africa observing cheetahs, elephants, giraffes, leopards, lions, and zebras in their natural habitats.

But, alas, this wonder is not to be. In its absence, however, Mother Nature has thoughtfully made an alternative available. Today, people can personally experience nature's beauty and wonder simply by looking at pictures. And what pictures they are! So, it seems to me, if people are going to spend so much time looking at pictures, they ought to be viewing things that elevate their minds, that *improve* them.

Thanks to such technologies as 4K cameras, remote recording, and aerial drones with cameras, nature photographers are able to obtain intimate high-definition close-ups and aerial shots that thrill and excite us while, simultaneously, expanding our consciousness.

The miraculous outcome? We can see the world through *the eyes of the wild.*

Imagine, we can sit comfortably at our desk, or lounge on a couch, while the manifold wonders of nature unfold before our very eyes. This is epoch-making! Charles Darwin circumnavigated the globe, looking at everything there was to see, but he could never see what we can, sitting at home watching pictures on screens.

It's almost as if we're gazing at nature through the eyes of God. I ask, does not this great privilege impose a great responsibility? If we have been permitted to see things through the eyes of God, should we not then act Godlike?

By now, I expect you've come to know me pretty well. I'm audacious if nothing else. So, here's my plan for how we can act Godlike. I've made it as easy and simple as possible.

The Plan

Our precious treasure trove of nature documentaries can and should be *politicized* for all it's worth. It should be *weaponized.* Here's how.

The 50th anniversary of Earth Day will occur on April 22, 2020. Much will be made of this event, which I view as a heaven-sent opportunity to relaunch the environmental revolution. To this end, I urge Earth Day 2020 organizers to make viewing of these nature documentaries a central focus of the anniversary celebration worldwide.

Earth Day organizers should promote showings of these documentaries by schools, churches, libraries, service clubs, and art and science museums. And, of course, television networks should be encouraged to rebroadcast these films and to publicize the broadcasts as their participation in the Earth Day celebration.

Look at the fabulous asset we've got to deploy. To start with, a great many great nature documentaries have been produced in recent decades. While BBC leads the way in producing this art, many other videos have been produced by *Animal Planet*, Discovery Channel, by *Disney Nature,* and by National Geographic. Plus, there's the *PBS NATURE* series, one of the most watched documentary film series on public television.

Glory be, this treasure trove of nature documentaries is readily available for viewing most anywhere for free or at low cost. There are 200 on *YouTube* alone. And all the episodes of NATURE are available on PBS. For Netflix subscribers, hundreds of titles are available, including all the BBC and National Geographic nature documentaries.

The aim, of course, is to create an implacable determination on the part of people everywhere to halt the further destruction of nature. After all, in politics, implacable determination is worth its weight in gold. Now, let's get down to brass tacks.

What's up next? The Presidential Election in 2020

Earth Day's 50th anniversary will be followed by a Presidential election six months later in November 2020. My, oh, my, this is convenient! Between the two events, there's a chance to make history.

In 2020, climate change won't be on the ballot, but the political purveyors of climate denial will be. Let's blow 'em to smithereens, I say!

I propose that the target audience for this outreach be Generation Y, the millennials, (people born during the 1980s and early 1990s) and Generation Z (people born between 1996-2010).

Why have I targeted these groups?

- Because younger people believe — overwhelmingly — that climate change is real, that humans are causing it, and that their own futures are gravely imperiled. (Worth noting, this includes *67 percent of all Republican voters aged 18-34.*)

- Because in the 2020 election Generations Y and Z will constitute almost 40 percent of the electorate. *But will they turn out to vote?* That's the 64 million-dollar question.

I think they will if they've viewed these awe-inspiring documentaries. After all, they'll simply be *doing what comes naturally*. Again, we are *programmed* to revere the wild. Mother Nature waves her magic wand; and, instantaneously, we are under her spell.

Let's *politicize* this reverence. If we do, young people will flood the polling places on Election Day in 2020 and throw the climate-denying rascals out. Oh, and by the way, in the process the dear, old, corrupt, and discredited political system will be *restored, revived, and renewed.*

"*What a great essay!
In Facilitating the Inevitable,
Byron Kennard shares with us how
the magic of Earth Day happened.
I was reminded of how exhilarating it was
to be a community organizer lucky enough to be present
at the birth of a new social movement.*"

— **Sam Love**, *Southern Coordinator, Earth Day 1970*

"*Byron was the initial wave
that turned into the tidal wave
of the Earth Day effort.
The Earth is thankful for his efforts. Me too!*"

— **Barbara Reid Alexander**, *Midwest Coordinator, Earth
Day 1970*

7

Facilitating the Inevitable

Once upon a time, I helped make the world a better place — the *whole* world too — not just some little piece of it, like a neighborhood or a town, or even a big chunk, like a continent. I am talking here about *the entire bloomin' planet.* And pulling this miracle off wasn't all that much trouble either. That's the good part. Mostly all I had to do was show up.

Sure, this happened a long time ago; and, ever since, I've been trudging through life, sweating and straining, like any other poor schmuck. But I have no gripe coming. Hey, I'm a guy who helped create *environmentalism.* I'm a guy who helped unleash a powerful worldwide force for good. And it was easier than falling off a log.

I'm talking about the time in the 1960s when I worked as a community organizer for the Conservation Foundation helping to form local civic groups to combat air and water pollution. This was the best — and easiest — job I ever had. Everything I touched turned to gold. I could do no wrong.

What I did doesn't *sound* easy. After all, I was asking people to serve as a *volunteer* in a high-minded struggle against tremendous odds. *What gall I had then!* Imagine, I was asking people to *contribute* their time, their energy, and, often, their money to a cause above and beyond their self-interest. *The miracle is that almost nobody turned me down!*

Jesus, I was good! (I *must* have been, right?)

Here's how it worked. I'd fly to some town — say, Milwaukee — get off the plane, and start running around, knocking on doors. I'd start by contacting leaders of local conservation groups concerned with fish, wildlife, parks, recreation, and so forth. And then I'd go after civic leaders working to improve the city's transportation, energy, food, and housing systems.

Putting all these things together in one context was a new thing back then — a new thing we called *environmentalism*. And, at the time, this new thing appealed to a lot of people, especially citizens who were civic-minded and who were volunteers in one local community group or another.

To this end, I recruited women's organizations like the League of Women Voters and the Junior League; public health groups like local affiliates of the American Lung Association; labor unions like the United Automobile Workers; and scientists too, especially high school biology teachers. I signed up Boy Scouts and Girl Scouts. I signed up student activists on local college campuses who were the vanguard of the then-burgeoning Sixties counterculture. A host of newly minted hippies enrolled on the spot.

The miracle kept on unfolding. When I left Milwaukee, I left behind a new broad-based regional civic coalition to fight environmental pollution. *Clean Air for Milwaukee!* Mission accomplished! Tomorrow, Atlanta, Charleston, Chicago, Denver, Louisville, Miami, San Antonio — all cities where I helped organize citizen opposition to environmental pollution.

Boy, was I impressed with myself then! I thought I was hot stuff. What vanity! I'm older and wiser now. Looking back at those halcyon days, I can see that I was in the enviable position of *being paid to facilitate the inevitable.*

In the 1960s, environmental protection was *an idea whose time had come.* Nothing was going to stop it. The environmental movement — like the big bang — was going to explode into existence no matter what. Then on April 22, 1970, Earth Day, *that's what happened!* And all the citizen groups I'd organized in the 60s turned out in full force to provide a backbone for the event.

Oh, how I wish I were a miracle worker who could recreate this glorious environmental history, but I'm not. Instead, I'm here to assert that nobody — certainly, not me — organized the environmental movement. The environmental movement organized itself. How that happens, I don't know. I'm just a mere mortal. All I know for sure is that Mother Nature was finagling behind the scenes to make miracles happen, pulling strings and eliminating barriers.

It's no wonder I could do no wrong back in those days. God was on my side! Or — as I prefer to describe it — *Mother Nature* was on my side. *No!* That's *not* right either! *I was on Mother Nature's side.*

She activated a divine spark in me that will forever bind me to her. And she lit a spark in countless others too. *She lit sparks all over the world!* She used her magic wand to summon a powerful new social movement into being. I've got to hand it to the old girl. She's one hell of an organizer!

"When Nature has work to be done," Ralph Waldo Emerson once observed, "she creates a genius to do it." Here's my version of Emerson's quote: "When Nature has work to be done, she creates a social movement to do it."

*"When one tugs at a single
thing in nature, he finds it
attached to the rest of the
world."*

— John Muir

8

Everything Really is Connected to Everything Else

The most significant consequence of Earth Day was not that it voiced a massive public demand for the control of environmental pollution, though that's how it started.

The most significant consequence of Earth Day was not that it launched a worldwide social movement on behalf of the preservation of nature, though that's what soon followed.

The most significant consequence of Earth Day was that it promulgated the ecological worldview.

I believe the ecological worldview is as consequential as any new idea *ever* introduced into society. I believe it could not *be more consequential.*

Look, I know some people will find this assertion to be preposterous, stupefying, or, at least, wildly exaggerated. Where do I find the gall it takes to make it? Easy! This worldview is entirely based on the First Law of Ecology: *everything is connected to everything else.*

If this idea is new to you, please let it soak in.

If everything *really is connected* to everything else, what does it signify? Well, I say it turns the old world upside down and inside out. I say it envelops and transforms our conceptions of politics, law, government, economics, business, industry, art, science, education, morality, ethics, and even religion — *especially* religion.

To understand, let's go back to Square One.

What is ecology?

All organisms, no matter their size, their species, or where they live, need to interact with other organisms in their neighborhood and with their environment in order to survive. Ecology is the scientific study of the interactions between organisms and their environment. The term comes from the Greek 'study of house', or the study of the place we live in.

History of Ecology

Where and when did the ecological idea originate? No one can say with any certainty, but there's some history to cite.

The origins of ecology are traceable back to the work of Swedish botanist Carolus Linnaeus (1707-1778), the father of modern taxonomy, the science of identifying and naming species. If one looks closely at nature, Linnaeus argued, one sees that even the simplest organisms play an important part in the functioning of natural systems. He declared that no living thing is useless.

Another key figure was the German explorer and scientist Alexander von Humboldt (1769-1859). Humboldt insisted that the only way to understand nature's complexity was to take accurate measurements in the field and then search for general laws. He believed that nothing in nature could be studied in isolation, that all phenomena were connected.

Certainly, the origins of modern ecology can be detected in the work of Charles Darwin (1809-1882). In his book, *On the Origin of Species*, published in 1859, Darwin proposed the theory of *natural selection,* which provided a mechanism for understanding how different species evolve. Darwin's work laid the foundation for the emergence of ecology as a distinct discipline during the latter part of the nineteenth century. It was then viewed as a subset of biology.

That's where *ecology* came from. Where did the so-called *First Law of Ecology* come from?

The First Law of Ecology — "everything is connected to everything else" — was first proclaimed by Barry Commoner (1917 - 2012) in his 1971 bestselling book, *The Closing Circle.* Commoner, a biology professor and founder of the Center for the Biology of Natural Systems at Washington University in St. Louis, was one of the world's best-known ecologists, famous for his spirited campaigns against nuclear testing, chemical pollution, and environmental decay.

The Closing Circle was one of the first books to bring the idea of sustainability to a mass audience. In it, Commoner proclaimed what is probably his most lasting legacy, the four laws of ecology:

1. *Everything is connected to everything else.* There is one ecosphere for all living organisms — what affects one, affects all.

2. *Everything must go somewhere.* There is no "waste" in nature — there is no "away" to which things can be thrown.

3. *Nature knows best.* Humankind has fashioned technology to improve upon nature, but such change in a natural system is likely to be detrimental to that system.

4. *There is no such thing as a free lunch.* Exploitation of nature will inevitably involve the conversion of resources from useful to useless forms.

Simon Butler, writing in the *Green Left Weekly*, describes how the First Law operates: "if any part of a natural ecosystem is damaged or overstressed, it can trigger far wider problems. For example, the burning of fossil fuels is overloading the global carbon cycle, which in turn is triggering dramatic changes to climate, global ice cover, weather patterns, ocean acidification, farming yields, sea levels, government budgets, and worldwide refugee figures. Any society that ignores Commoner's first law invites ecological and social turmoil."

I've written this book to prove that you can't fool Mother Nature. Now I'm writing to prove that you can't evade the First Law of Ecology.

The Environmental Revolution & The Ecological Worldview

My long association with environmentalism and ecology (and their intricate interactions) did not originate in anything I can brag about (much as I'd like to).

In 1970, I was a left-wing political activist, cast in the mold of Sixties counterculture. My passionate focus was on combatting the pollution of the environment by big business. If, on Earth Day, you had asked me what I hoped the event would accomplish, I would have said to put CEOs of polluting corporations in jail.

Frankly, I didn't know my ass from a hole in the ground about *ecology*. I'd never even heard the word. So, I've got Barry Commoner to thank. He provided me with one hell of an education and in one hell of a short time.

I embraced the ecological worldview wholeheartedly. It became the perspective from which I view and interpret everything that's going on around me. The ecological worldview is my guiding light. And it gives me the gall it takes to make even more audacious claims about the historical significance of the environmental revolution.

OKAY, NOW, LET'S RANSACK HISTORY

There's something you should know about me. I've had my nose stuck in a history book practically since I learned to read. And what drives my interest in history is what drives my interest in community organizing. If you're searching for ways to make the world a better place, what the hell actually works?!

In this search, I've ransacked history's attic, history's closets, history's backstairs, and history's basement.

Think of it this way: I've read hundreds of history books, so you don't have to! Nice of me, huh? And now I'm going to shamelessly exploit everything I've learned to score points, to convince you that the environmental revolution I helped foment represents a major turning point in history, as momentous as any that ever occurred before.

To buttress this claim, the three essays that follow compare the environmental revolution to other transformative epochs in history: specifically, the Renaissance, the Protestant Reformation, and the French Revolution.

You won't be surprised to learn that, in each of these comparisons, my green buddies and I come out smelling like roses. (Which is appropriate, don't you think?)

9

The Renaissance:
Everything Old is New Again

The Renaissance (a French word meaning *rebirth*) revived the ideas, values, art, and architecture associated with the greatness of ancient Greece and Rome. Renaissance thinkers believed they could restore a lost link to the cultures of Greece and Rome and bring about a "rebirth" of that greatness in their own time.

They succeeded magnificently. The Renaissance (ca. A.D. 1300-1600) was perhaps the most profound advance in civilization since the fall of ancient Rome.

In restoring this link, the Renaissance brought about an explosion of new cultural, economic, scientific, and intellectual changes that shattered old ways of thinking and pushed civilization onto a higher level.

The Rebirth of Humanism

The grandest accomplishment of Renaissance thinkers was the promulgation and embrace of *humanism*.

Humanism downplays religious dogma. It makes the dignity and worth of the individual the principal focus. In the order of things, it places humans front and center. The mantra of Renaissance thinkers was "Man is the measure of all things," a precept they borrowed from Protagoras, the Greek philosopher.

For example, the Renaissance revived classical ideas about the key role of citizenship, which had been latent since the days of Greek democracy and the Roman republic. People began to conceive of themselves as possessing intrinsic *rights*. Imagine that!

A new spirit of inquisitiveness pervaded society. In the Middle Ages, society was focused on the church, religion, and salvation. The Renaissance saw the emergence of a humanist philosophy that emphasized reason, scientific inquiry, and human fulfillment in the course of existence here on earth. In short, the Renaissance represents the transition from the Middle Ages to the modern world.

The Renaissance & the Environmental Revolution

I argue that what the Renaissance did for humanism, the Environmental Revolution did for nature.

Environmentalists believed they could restore a lost link to the ancient world's reverence for nature and its focus on the individual's direct experience of the natural world. *In the order of things, environmentalism places humanity's relationship to nature front and center.*

It was as if we needed reminding that Mother Nature is in charge of things. Earth Day jogged our memory. In a way, Earth Day summoned us back home, back to the nest in which we were nurtured, back to the cradle in which our species came to flourish.

Environmentalism, like the Renaissance, also brought about an explosion of cultural, economic, scientific, and intellectual change that shattered old ways of thinking and pushed civilization onto a higher level. The Environmental Revolution heralded the transition from the Industrial Age to the post-industrial age.

The Renaissance produced revolutionary changes in politics, government, economics, and science; and, in doing so, it relied on cultural change — specifically on the arts, literature, and architecture. I contend that the Environmental Revolution did the same thing.

The Renaissance sought to forge conscious connections between humanity and the cosmos — and it *succeeded*. I contend that the Environmental Revolution did the same thing.

Both the Renaissance and the Environmental Revolution concerned themselves with spiritual concerns of human beings. As I see it, environmentalism revived the spirit of such ancient natured-centered belief systems as paganism, theism, pantheism, and deism. These focus on the individual's connection with the natural world and with reverence for it.

The religion of Native Americans, for example, was often celebrated and cited in defense of environmentalism, as was Buddhism for its keen focus on nature. And there's Hinduism in India and Shintoism in Japan, both of which are rooted in nature worship.

It's interesting to note that, following Earth Day, there was a major resurgence of the "back to the land" movement, a phenomenon that keeps repeating down through history. These movements manifest a fervor that is akin to religion.

History books, which are full of dark deeds and dread accounts of human misadventures, also contain some bright chapters. Here I've recited two of them. The Renaissance served the cause of humanity. The Environmental Revolution served the cause of nature. And because everything *really is* connected to everything else, these two grand epochs share a link in history.

10

Me & Martin Luther

Okay, as you're well aware; so far, I've bragged shamelessly about how my favorite revolution — the one I helped organize — accomplished miracles for the human race.

I've described how environmentalism upgraded civilization, promoted social justice, and enriched the culture — in addition, of course, to making great strides in environmental protection. But here's where I go for broke. Here's where I describe my career as *a religious reformer.*

Back in the 1960s, when I became an environmentalist, I had no idea that I'd wind up a religious reformer. Who would have guessed it? *Not me!* (My mother, if she hears of it, will be spinning in her grave.)

I wasn't even *religious!* Besides, at the time, I had my hands full trying to handle my responsibilities as Mother Nature's emissary here on Earth, as a fomenter of political revolution, and as a modern-day Renaissance man.

Nevertheless, I spent decades passionately advocating the ecological worldview, which, if properly understood, turns the old-world upside down — and that includes the world of religion.

Thus, I claim, when it comes to reforming religion, the Environmental Revolution is — in its way — the equal of the Protestant Reformation. Why? Because the Reformation challenged fundamental religious ideas that had been dominant for thousands of years. The Environmental Revolution, in its way, has done the same thing.

Maybe that's why I feel such affinity for Martin Luther, a pioneering defender of truth and religious freedom. I think of Luther as a sort of soul brother. In a way, he and I trod the same path. Here's his side of the story.

Martin Luther Nails It!

Martin Luther (1483-1546) was a German monk who in 1517 launched the Protestant Reformation by nailing a document on the door of Wittenberg's Castle Church — his famous *95 Theses*. Luther changed the course of Western history for the better — he's my kind of guy.

Luther's postulations denied some basic teachings of Catholicism, especially the belief that the Church — and *only* the Church — was the route to salvation.

For a thousand years, the Church claimed to be the intermediary between God and the individual; and, in the 15th century, this claim was widely accepted. Most everyone believed that only priests could grant redemption, and all the poor wretches who lacked it were doomed to burn in Hell.

Luther turned the Church's teaching on its ear. He taught instead that faith was a personal matter that could be developed and practiced without the medium of the Church. The Bible,

Luther argued, is the supreme religious authority, not the Pope. Through the Bible, each individual can find a path to salvation on his or her own.

The liberating force of Luther's ideas on the people of his time can scarcely be imagined. For an eon, they'd been taught that God was off-limits to ordinary mortals. Now they could seek salvation on their own. To sum it up, the Protestant Reformation fundamentally altered the view that people had of themselves in relation to the *Creator*.

Fast Forward to the 20th Century

Here's where I get off comparing environmentalism to the Reformation. Environmentalism fundamentally altered the view people have of themselves in relation to *Natural Creation*.

For a thousand years (or more), people have been taught that humanity is the crown of natural creation, the highest, grandest expression of divine intent. Creation is a pyramid — so we've long been told — with humanity perched on top of everything else. And, conveniently for us, the remainder of natural creation — the birds and the bees, the coal and the oil, the gold and the uranium, *everything* — exists primarily for human use and exploitation.

Then, in 1970, along came Earth Day to promote an idea that totally invalidates the pyramid scheme: *ecology*. Ecology reveals that natural systems consist of complex, interdependent webs within which all life forms are embedded; and, in which, all life forms are equal.

In contrast, the Bible asserts man's dominion over nature and embraces the doctrine of *anthropocentrism* — the view that humanity is the center of existence. This view is mistaken and dangerously so. What we need is a new religion, which recognizes that human survival requires profound changes in how we perceive our place in the planetary ecosystem.

To me, the ecological worldview provides the basis for this religion. The new religion would replace anthropocentrism with *ecocentrism,* a nature-centered system of values. Ecocentrism incorporates respect and reverence for *all* species of life. It makes the crown of creation not man but nature.

Ecocentrism *is* a new way of perceiving ourselves in relation to the planetary ecosystem. It looks at the ecosphere as a whole, not just at the part that is human. Ponder this quote from the late Stan Rowe, a geo-ecologist, who was Professor of Plant Ecology at the University of Saskatchewan and the author of *Earth Alive: Essays on Ecology:*

"The ecocentric argument is grounded in the belief that, compared to the undoubted importance of the human part, the whole ecosphere is even more significant and consequential: more inclusive, more complex, more integrated, more creative, more beautiful, more mysterious, and older than time."

Me & Martin Luther, Really?!

Okay, so my claim to be a religious reformer doesn't exactly put me on a peer level with Martin Luther. But I can rub elbows with him, can't I? At least a little?

The truth is we Earth Day organizers thought of ourselves much more as political reformers than as moral reformers. But we did at least let the ecological cat out of the philosophical bag. In all earnestness, we proclaimed the sacredness of nature and the moral responsibility of the individual to take direct personal action to protect it.

And — come to think of it — in effect, we nailed our Ecological Theses — not on the door of a church — but on the door of the US Capitol. Doesn't this make me a teensy-weensy little bit like Martin Luther?

> *"Any religion old or new,*
> *that stressed the magnificence of the universe*
> *as revealed by modern science,*
> *might be able to draw forth reserves of reverence*
> *and awe hardly tapped by the conventional faiths.*
> *Sooner or later, such a religion will emerge."*
>
> **Carl Sagan**, *Pale Blue Dot (1994)*

11

Liberty, Equality, Diversity

Everyone knows the French national motto, 'n'est-ce pas'? I mean, who hasn't heard the phrase, *Liberté, Égalité, Fraternité,* at one time or another? Just three little words — but each one embodying a concept potent enough to bring down a thousand-year-old absolute monarchy.

Whatever you think of the French Revolution — "it was the best of times; it was the worst of times" — you've got to agree it was one of the most zealous efforts in history to achieve social justice. The revolution was a crucial turning point in civilization, an event of almost unparalleled significance.

Now, ma chérie, don't get your knickers in a twist, but I'm here to argue that the Environmental Revolution signified pretty much the same thing. I'm arguing that social justice is *intrinsic* to the ecological worldview.

Okay, *okay!* I grant you. The cause of environmental protection and the cause of social justice are not normally thought of as being similar — or even compatible. If anything, environmentalism and social justice are thought of as being in competition, or even at odds. *Mon Dieu!* This view could not be more mistaken!

Still, I know this audacious assertion takes some explaining. Indeed, it necessitates a brief tour of French history.

Come along! I promise you it won't be a bore.

Before the French Revolution, concepts of liberty and equality were hard even to imagine. The French people were subjects of an absolute monarch who ruled by divine right. All legislative, judicial, and executive powers were in the King's hands. He exercised final authority in all matters, including the power of life and death over his subjects.

Society was a rigid hierarchy headed by the monarch. Under the monarch were the nobility and religious officials (2-3 percent of the population). At the bottom of the hierarchy were the peasants (90 percent of the population). In between was a small middle class consisting of merchants, craftsmen, and tradesmen.

In 1789, the revolution erupted and blew the lid off this antiquated structure.

Equality & The Ecological Worldview

The revolution abolished the old regime's legal structure, which was grounded in an acceptance of — indeed, a dedication to — inequality before the law. *The Declaration of the Rights of Man* proclaimed by the revolution made *all* citizens equal before the law, a throughly radical proposition in those days.

For centuries, there had been different sets of laws in France, one, for nobles and another for peasants. For instance, it was illegal for peasants to hunt or fish. They couldn't even hunt the rabbits or birds that were eating their crops. This game was protected for the nobility's hunting expeditions. It was even illegal for peasants to cut down a tree to get firewood. A peasant caught doing so was punished with death.

Pity the poor peasants! For a thousand years, the Church had taught them that social inequality was God's plan, and it was His Divine Will that they submit to it meekly and without complaint. And so long as the peasants complied, the nobility could wallow in its wealth and privileges without worrying about rebels breaking into their castles and slitting their throats. When the revolution came along and wised up the peasants, they did rebel and started breaking into castles and slitting noble throats.

Now, let's shift gears and consider another turning point in history — one that's not quite so gruesome. Unlike the French Revolution, the Environmental Revolution did not include a Reign of Terror. (Though sometimes I think it *should have*.) But the similarities between the two are immense.

People had always been taught that the whole of natural creation was a pyramid with humans (rightfully) at the peak of it, lording it over the rest of nature.

Beneath humans were other life forms — the animal species, right down to the tiniest insect. The pyramid of life rested, of course, on all the planet's natural resources — water and air, oceans and forests, coal, oil and gas deposits, precious metals: silver, gold, and uranium — to exploit and so on, *ad infinitum*.

Now, imagine, people were taught that God Himself had organized all this planetary plentitude for mankind's use, benefit and exploitation. It was *His* plan.

In 1970, however, Earth Day came along and promulgated a radically different idea. Earth Day proclaimed *the ecological worldview.* In this view, natural creation is seen as an infinite series of complex, interdependent webs in which all life forms — including *homo sapiens* — are inextricably embedded.

There are no hierarchies in nature. In a web, all inhabitants are equal, and all contribute to the whole. It's all thanks to Mother Nature. The dear old girl is a fervent democrat.

Liberty & The Ecological Worldview

In complex, interdependent webs there is no one on top dominating and controlling everyone else. This is simply because *there is no top*.

Moreover, in webs every component has a function to perform *and it must be at liberty to perform its function*. The health of the overall system depends on it.

If something comes along that deprives a component of its liberty, then the entire system can become dysfunctional. Insects, for example, are not to be despised but revered for the crucial role they play in planetary ecology. Now, if human beings are foolish enough to deprive insects of their life and liberty, agriculture would soon collapse; and, before long, most humans would starve to death.

I argue that in nature, liberty is an inherent quality. I say, long live the bugs, not the King!

Fraternity & The Ecological Worldview

This brings us to fraternity, and here's where I have a minor objection to the French national motto.

Fraternité doesn't cut the mustard, not anymore. I propose dropping it and substituting instead the word, *diversité.* That's French, of course, for diversity; so, my revised version would read: Liberté, Égalité, Diversité, or in plain English: Liberty, Equality, Diversity.

Here's why I think this change would be a good idea. The word "fraternity" describes the state or feeling of friendship and mutual support within a group; but, for my money, it smacks too much of *brotherhood.* When most people think of fraternity, they think of Sigma Chi. That will, of course, not do. In this day and age, we must emphatically embrace *sisterhood* too, and that's just for starters.

Fraternity has to do with the relationships of man to man, which is fine as far as it goes. But it doesn't go far enough, not nearly. Diversity goes *all the way.* Diversity has to do with the relationships of man to all life forms — to animals, to trees and forests, to oceans and seas, to space and all it contains, and ultimately to the cosmos.

Nature's loving embrace of diversity in all its forms provides the strongest possible justification for civil rights and liberties for all people. It is Mother Nature's rebuke to oppression, inequality, and bigotry. The dear old girl — in addition to being a fervent democrat — is also a revolutionary.

So, I say, vive la révolution de l'environnement!

> *"Alarmist rhetoric about
> the future of our environment
> has the tendency to immobilize us.
> Byron Kennard's essay,
> Edmund Burke's Earth Day Speech,
> is a refreshing siren of sanity."*
>
> — **James Kirchick**, *Visiting Fellow, Brookings Institution*
>
> ---
>
> *"Kennard's essay on Edmund Burke is brilliant.
> Creative and spirited!"*
>
> — **Carl Pope,** *former CEO and Chair of the Sierra
> Club*

12

Edmund Burke's Earth Day Speech

How Environmentalists became Burkeans
and Burkeans became Environmentalists

Here's my favorite quote from Edmund Burke's Earth Day speech, "Never, no, never did Nature say one thing and Wisdom another." Isn't that terrific? And so apt for the occasion! I couldn't have said it better myself.

What's that you say? Edmund Burke didn't make an Earth Day speech! He couldn't have! Earth Day was in 1970, almost 200 years after Burke died. That's true, of course; but, nevertheless, there he was — big as life — seated next to me on the speakers' platform. Funny, but what struck me as strange was Burke's speaking at all. Why was Edmund Burke — of all people — addressing an Earth Day rally? Talk about a fish out of water!

Edmund Burke is regarded as the founder of modern conservatism, and Earth Day 1970 was a high-water mark of the then prevalent left-wing counterculture. My own remarks for the occasion, for example, were a savage attack on big business polluters in which I advocated mandatory life sentences for corporate CEOs.

More strangeness was to follow. When Burke began speaking, I — along with the huge crowd listening — was soon mesmerized by his magnificent eloquence. Speaking of nature's bounty, Burke urged Americans "not to commit waste on the inheritance . . . hazarding to leave to those who come after them, a ruin instead of a habitation."

(What a phrase maker! "A ruin instead of a habitation" . . . I was blown away. That Edmund Burke is one heck of a guy. No wonder he's got devoted followers the world over who proudly proclaim themselves Burkeans.)

As he went on, I realized Burke was describing a coherent, overall approach to environmental protection, one that was simple, powerful, and persuasive. Then it occurred to me — hey, man! — this is Burkean environmentalism. Here's what it boils down to:

The Primacy of Prudence

It's highly imprudent, Burke warned, for humans to radically intervene in the functioning of natural systems whose boundless complexity and infinite interdependence exceed our understanding. Such interventions are especially unwise and dangerous when these systems — such as climate — underpin our very existence. Plaintively, Burke asked what in past human experience suggests that such large-scale meddling is harmless? On the contrary, it's prudent to assume that great risks are involved.

(In his remarks, Burke acclaimed prudence as "the chief among virtues." So I wanted to be absolutely sure of the word's exact meaning. I checked the dictionary: prudence is the exercise of careful good judgment based on actual past experience and the application of such judgment to show care for the future.)

When it comes to politics and government, Burke argued that prudence — simple, ordinary prudence — in itself provides a sound base for public policy on the environment. And because this is self-evidently true, environmental activists can stand and fight on this base with strength and confidence.

The Desirability of Organic Change

Burke made clear that his call for prudence is not a call to halt progress. He believes that change is desirable, necessary; and, in any case, nature compels it. "We must all obey the great law of change," he declared. "It is the most powerful law of nature, and the means perhaps of its conservation." The challenge, he said, is how best to manage change.

Burke believes the answer to this challenge may be found in the functioning of natural systems. Change must be sought organically. Organic change occurs on a small scale, incrementally, from the bottom up. It evolves without being forced or contrived.

Organic change should characterize environmental politics too. Burke said change in nature was "a condition of unchangeable constancy, (that) moves on through the varied tenor of perpetual decay, fall, renovation and progression. Thus, by preserving the method of nature in the conduct of the state, in what we improve, we are never wholly new; in what we retain, we are never wholly obsolete." At this point, Burke's oratory had me swooning.

In this connection, Burke heaped praise on the thousands of new small green businesses and entrepreneurial endeavors now flourishing throughout the country. These businesses are not only transforming the economy, he said, they are also forming a vibrant and vocal political constituency. (Hearing this, I thought — wow! — a constituency like this is exactly what Burkean environmentalism needs if its promise is to be realized.)

When Burke finished speaking, he received a prolonged standing ovation, and then I led the crowd in a rousing version of "For He's a Jolly Good Fellow!" Indeed, this version was so rousing that it woke me up. The whole thing had been a dream! But it was a dream worth reflecting on, that's for sure.

I realized that, in my dream, all Burke had done was to trot out the arguments he'd made in *Reflections on the French Revolution* (1790) and apply them to the planetary ecological crisis. This book, his most famous work, was written to express Burke's profound hostility to the revolution's spirit of total, radical innovation.

It is said that a man of discernment who studies the past can predict the future. That's a good description of Edmund Burke. In 1790, when most others were cheering the French on, he foresaw a breakdown of social order; and, presciently, he predicted the coming of the Reign of Terror and the military dictatorship that followed, which instigated twenty-three years of European warfare and led to four million deaths.

As Burke saw it, the revolutionaries were violently dismantling a social system that had slowly evolved and endured for over a thousand years. Worse yet, they were dismantling it practically overnight. The zealous French revolutionaries were convinced they could build a new and better society from scratch; so, they gleefully threw the proverbial baby out with the bathwater.

Here's the green Burkean take on this: if it is unwise and dangerous to make radical innovations in social systems that have evolved and endured for millennia, then how much more unwise and dangerous is it to make radical innovations in natural systems that evolved and endured over eons?

Farmer Burke

How did Burke's environmentalism come to him? It came naturally. Look at his life story. He was Irish, a commoner. He wasn't rich. These were major disadvantages in the world he inhabited. There was little or no chance he could become a minister of state. He could serve in parliament only as the beneficiary of a wealthy, aristocratic patron who could secure him a seat.

Burke yearned to overcome these disadvantages by becoming "a gentleman." In his time, being a gentleman meant owning land, a lot of land. So, in 1768, Burke borrowed heavily to purchase a 600-acre country estate. The estate, a working farm, was near Beaconsfield in Buckinghamshire about 25 miles west of London. Given his indebtedness, Burke had to make the farm pay. To this end, he became "Farmer Burke"; and, in doing so, he was true to himself. He sought the lessons that past experience has taught humans.

Burke talked to local families who had long been farmers. After his death, his literary executors, French Laurence and Walker King, wrote this about Farmer Burke: ". . . he was principally guided by the traditionary skill and experience of that class of men, who, from father to son, have for generations labored in calling forth the fertility of the English soil."

Way back then, Burke was seeking to understand sustainable farming.

Today, Burke is remembered for his political achievements, his ideas, his literary gifts. His intimate association with the land is overlooked. It should not be. Laurence and King also wrote this about Farmer Burke: "He not only found in agriculture the most agreeable relaxation from his more serious cares, but he regarded the cultivation of the earth, and the improvement of all which it produces, as a sort of moral and religious duty."

I argue that, for Burke, nature offered a living model of how best to manage change in politics and society. I'm not alone in this view. It is strongly buttressed by Yuval Levin, author of *The Great Debate: Edmund Burke, Thomas Paine, and the Birth of Right and Left.*

According to Levin, a devout Burkean, Burke had in mind "the example of biological systems transmitting their traits through the generations, a system of inheritance that he saw replicated in human society." Levin argues that this gave Burke a focus on "the facts of birth and death and the need to manage change, decay, renovation and progress." Politics + ecology: Levin got this right.

Given Levin's input, I can't claim to have cooked up Burkean environmentalism on my own, much as I'd like to. I also owe primary thanks to Amol Rajan, author of "Edmund Burke: How did a long dead Irishman become the hottest thinker of 2010?" This article in the British newspaper, *The Independent*, planted the idea of Burkean environmentalism in my mind, where it has been growing by leaps and bounds ever since.

In his article, Rajan makes much of Burke's statement that:

"Society is indeed a contract... [It is] a partnership not only between those who are living,
　　but between those who are living, those who are dead,
　　　　and those who are to be born."

Commenting on this passage, Rajan states: "On this analysis, the living rent the earth, but do not possess it; they are its temporary custodians, tasked with conserving a precious inheritance which will in turn become a future generation's precious inheritance." And then Rajan made this striking observation: "Very, very few environmentalists realise that this analysis presents Burke as their patron saint . . . a man who championed sustainability centuries before it was fashionable."

Then and there I decided to join these "very, very few" — to become a disciple of Burkean environmentalism.

Nowadays I'm seeking converts to the cause, but that's no problem — at least not when I'm having dreams about Earth Day. There converts show up en masse. Swayed by the power of Burke's language and reasoning, environmentalists become Burkeans and Burkeans become environmentalists. And we all live happily ever after.

13

Creative Destruction is Good for the Environment

Conservatives are enthralled by "creative destruction," the theory devised by Joseph Schumpeter (1883-1960), the Harvard economist and conservative icon. They regard it as one the great methods for improving society through the functioning of the market.

Creative destruction occurs when radical innovators devise new technologies that force large, established companies to adapt or die. The term refers to capitalism's ability to innovate, destroy, and then reinvent itself.

In this, capitalism is emulating nature. Natural ecosystems thrive on processes of continual creation and destruction. In winter, for example, nature kills off weak life forms, thus making space for new ones to take their place in spring.

Really, there are only two things the reader needs to know about creative destruction: (1) it's *creative* and (2) it's *destructive*. Typically, it's creative in the long run but destructive in the short run.

For example, technological breakthroughs like the steam engine or the telephone affected society positively in the long run but negatively in the short run. For blacksmiths or telegraph operators these breakthroughs were bad news. The poor buggers were thrown out of work.

Now, in describing creative destruction, Schumpeter chose to focus on its *creativity*. He saw creative destruction as the vehicle which actually moves resources from old and obsolescent uses to new and more efficient, productive ones.

Talk like this is music to my ears. Speaking as an environmentalist, I'm enthralled by creative destruction too. It's good for the environment! *And why wouldn't it be?* As I've argued, creative destruction emulates the processes of natural ecosystems.

Look, for example, at how the present boom in rooftop solar systems is challenging the electricity industry. Many homeowners are moving away from centralized power generation relying on fossil fuels and opting for distributed generation using renewables. And the current boom in clean technology is proving to be a fantastic engine for industrial growth and job creation as well as greenhouse gas reduction.

This is due to creative destruction, an unstoppable force now surging through all sectors of the vast energy industry. At the center of this turmoil is the coal industry, the focus of intense and confusing political conflict, where accusations of wrong-doing and counter accusations fly fast and furious, left and right.

Creative Destruction & The Coal Industry

Today the coal industry is swiftly declining, and there's no avoiding it. Coal is being replaced by better, cleaner, cheaper forms of energy — wind and solar power — and by energy efficiency upgrades that pay off in spades. That's all to the good; but, in the process, thousands of coal miners are being seriously and unfairly harmed.

Right-wing Republicans love to blame environmentalists for the industry's decline, claiming that the greens are waging "a war on coal." That's baloney. If there is "a war on coal," it is being waged by free market forces, not by environmentalists.

If they were genuine and honest free market advocates, these right-wingers would be leading the cheers for the collapse of the coal industry. They'd acknowledge that — thanks to the process of creative destruction — more technologically advanced energy resource industries will thrive and new economic growth and jobs will follow in their wake. And the icing on the cake will be a healthier, safer world to live in.

Now, if you ask me, I'd claim there's "a war on coal miners" being waged by the *owners* of coal mines. These fat cat plutocrats are behaving atrociously.

As the industry declines, coal companies are declaring bankruptcy in droves, eight alone in the past year. And, as they do, mine owners are not only depriving workers of their jobs, *they are reneging on their legal obligations to provide pensions and health care.* The result is catastrophic for thousands of working coal miners and for retired miners and their families.

(Bankruptcy proceedings, however, ensure that fat cats get fat bonuses as they walk out the door.)

A just and compassionate society would see to it that the people harmed by creative destruction through no fault of their own would receive assistance. But — forgive my cynicism — how often does society behave with justice and compassion? Nope, as history amply demonstrates, society celebrates and rewards winners profusely. But innocent people harmed by creative destruction are ignored, forgotten, and left to crawl off into some corner and die.

Can't we do better? We should — and not merely in the interests of justice and compassion but in the interests of social order and stability. It is good politics to soothe the resentments of those who are being screwed by the impersonal functions of the "free market."

In this situation, I think the government should step in and pay the miners their pensions and the costs of their health care. (In fact, that's exactly what the so-called "Green New Deal" proposes to do. It also would fund job training for workers in fossil fuel industries.)

The Politics of Creative Destruction

Imagine how the politics of social change would be altered and improved if society committed itself to the goal of providing a safety net for people dislodged from their livelihood by the impersonal market force of creative destruction.

Such a commitment could be justified simply as a reasonable price of progress. We want progress, and we want social order. Here's a way of pursuing progress without disrupting social order by creating masses of needy people, boiling over with resentment of their unfair treatment and eager to strike out at somebody — *anybody*. These masses are fodder for demagogues. (Need I say more?)

There's another political angle to this as well, one with strong appeal in this era of intense political polarization. As I noted, the concept of creative destruction is heartily embraced by many conservatives (those of the honest variety). Now, if social net provisions could be put in place, liberals and environmentalists could embrace creative destruction too.

Bear in mind that a technological innovation is neither a Democrat nor a Republican. *It's a tool!* If it solves an environmental problem, liberals should be happy. If it creates new jobs and economic growth, then conservatives should be happy.

So, let's spread the joy around! Creative destruction *is* good for the economy and for the environment too!

I think Professor Schumpeter would be pleased to learn how his seminal insight has endured and evolved. He must have been an engaging fellow. As a young man, he declared his intention to become a great lover, a great horseman, and a great economist. Later in life, he claimed that he'd achieved two out of the three but declined to reveal at which endeavor he'd failed. If I had the chance, I'd tell him, "No matter. Now you can claim to have been a great environmentalist as well."

"*The hero of Byron Kennard's book is small business. He claims that small business is perhaps the single best tool we possess for healing damaged natural systems. What's the basis for his audacious and unconventional claim? When the economy is damaged and in need of repair, it's generally acknowledged that small business entrepreneurs, step in to heal the damage by creating a multitude of new enterprises and new jobs.*

"*Byron argues that small business entrepreneurs can also heal the environment when it's damaged and in need of repair by creating a multitude of innovative solutions to environmental problems. To prove his point, Byron points to the thriving world of green entrepreneurship, a worldwide phenomenon producing miracles on a daily basis.*"

— **Marilyn D. Landis**, *President & CEO, Basic Business Concepts, Inc.; former Chair, National Small Business Association.*

14

The Irresistible Power of Self-Organizing Systems

Ecologists marvel at nature's self-organizing capacities, a spontaneous process whereby some form of beneficial order is created by individuals interacting without central coordination.

Think of flocks of birds flying in beautiful formations. There's an aerodynamic reason for this. Flocks sense and exploit changing wind patterns enabling them to use the surrounding air in the most energy efficient way, something an individual bird cannot do.

Think of honeybees swarming about industriously on a spring day. These bees are home-hunting. Swarming is how honeybee colonies reproduce themselves. In the process of swarming, the original colony reproduces to two and sometimes more colonies.

Think of fish *schooling*, that is, swimming in the same direction in a coordinated manner with the individual members precisely spaced from each other as they perform complicated maneuvers.

These animals are performing social functions that enable them to thrive and survive. These self-organizing groups are far better at foraging for food and at detecting predators than are individuals. And they accomplish these benefits without central direction.

Look at what nature has accomplished via self-organizing systems. New life forms pop up everywhere on their own — even in physical and chemical extremes that, until recently, were thought to preclude life.

Life in the form of microbes, algae, lichens, and fungi can be found in both the hottest deserts and in the coldest places on the planet. The acid hot springs in Yellowstone National Park are teeming with life. There are organisms that thrive inside the cooling water within nuclear reactors. There are bacteria that can endure high levels of radiation. Life has been found inside *rocks*.

To top it off, natural self-organizing systems are typically capable of self-renewal and self-repair when damaged. *That's extraordinary!* Golly, wouldn't it be great if such miraculous systems existed in *human* communities? Well, count your lucky stars! They do!

Like nature, small business is a self-organizing system.

Society fetes small businesses for many reasons, not the least of which is their function in self-correcting the market when something goes wrong. Small businesses possess this healing power because they are, unlike the Fortune 500, *self-organizing* — just like nature. Look at small business as a *system* and you'll see how closely it resembles the workings of nature. Both are complex, interdependent webs that are highly efficient, adaptive, ingenious, and resilient.

Here's how this resemblance between natural systems and small business plays out. Self-organizing systems can communicate with each other. They are capable of infinite sensitivity to each other's multifaceted dimensions. So, the best way to address a self-organizing system is through another self-organizing system. *Hot diggity!* This makes small business the best tool we've got to heal wounded natural systems.

Finally, there's the politics of this. A reliance on self-organizing systems is a conservative method of *social change*. What I've described is a conservative method of *environmental protection* — one that both conservatives and ecologists can agree on. Here is, at long last, an appealing and prudent basis for bipartisan political action.

15

Small Business: the Great Green Hope

Small business is society's best tool for addressing the planetary ecological crisis — ***the single best tool.***

How's that for an assertion? Most people I suspect — including most environmentalists — will think it preposterous. How can this be? After all, the crisis is global, and the businesses are small. What's the connection?

Small businesses, being small in scale, countless in number, utterly decentralized, and boundlessly diverse, are impossible to see as a whole. This doesn't mean they lack clout.

On the contrary, small business is one of the most powerful forces on earth. It's the glue that holds the economy together. That's why I'm fond of comparing small business to gravity, which actually is the most powerful force on earth. But we can't see gravity. It's invisible, like small business.

We owe gravity a lot. If there were no gravity, everything not stuck in place would start floating in the air— pens and papers located on your desk, your furniture, your car. Far worse, the air in the atmosphere would disappear into space as would the water in the oceans, rivers, and lakes. Egads!

Thank you, dear old gravity! Where would we be without you?! We appreciate your pulling for us!

We owe small business a lot too. If there were no small businesses, how would the economy recover from downturns? Economic history shows that each time a recession hits and blows everything to smithereens, small businesses come rushing to the rescue.

Thank you, small business people! Where would we be without you guys?! Mired in economic stagnation, that's where!

Small business as an engine of environmental protection

No doubt, you've heard small business acclaimed as "the engine of the economy," the source of most innovations and most new jobs. That's all true. But I'm writing to acclaim small business as an engine of environmental protection too. Here's why I call small business the great green hope: *The engine that's powerful enough to renew and restore a devastated economy is powerful enough to transform the economy into sustainability.*

Here's how this magic transpires.

• Small business's vaunted capacity for innovating is no mere piece of luck, no accident, no coincidence, and certainly no common or trivial thing. This capacity derives from qualities that are intrinsic to small-scale enterprise alone.

• Experimentation on the small scale, for example, is cheaper than on the large-scale. And it's also much safer. If a small-scale experiment fails, then not much is lost. If a small-scale experiment blows up, the damage is limited. In contrast large-scale institutions experiment on the large-scale, which is costly and often dangerous. Because they are, by definition, bureaucratic in nature, large-scale institutions lack the finesse of small businesses, which can float like a butterfly and sting like a bee.

• Here's the heart of the matter: the economy was not called into being by any central authority, whether royal or imperial, democratic or dictatorial. No! The economy was formed over time through countless actions by countless actors. Its formation was not coordinated and, indeed, *could not be coordinated.*

• The only way in which the economy can now be *transformed* into sustainability *is in the way it was formed in the first place:* that is, through countless acts by countless actors over time.

• Top-down, command and control approaches by big government cannot effect this transformation. They are too clumsy, too heavy-handed, and too easily confounded and defeated by the boundless complexity, both of the environment and of the economy. (And, damn it all, on top of that, *everything is connected to everything else!* Holy cow! What's a central planner to do?!)

• Like nature, the economy is multi-faceted beyond belief. But, thanks to the capaciousness of organic change, the economy's every facet can actually be encompassed by one small-scale enterprise or other. Some entrepreneur, out on the prowl, will detect the facet, examine it, and try to turn a profit by improving it. Large-scale institutions, of course, are utterly incapable of this responsiveness; capaciousness is not their bag.

• In any case, command and control approaches by big government now elicit such fervent political opposition that they're not in the cards. The enduring savagery of political polarization negates the possibility.

• May God forgive me for saying so, but I honestly believe that there's a better chance of civilization collapsing due to catastrophic climate change than there is of the national government making a vigorous, all-out mobilization to combat the crisis. Yep, it's *that bad*.

• The option left on the table — to me, the best option — is to rely on organic change, operating through the medium of small-scale enterprise, to do the job. Organic change is neither planned nor designed. It doesn't depend on victories at the election polls or in the halls of Congress. It evades political polarization. It succeeds through stealth. Thank heaven, I say, this option is on the table! *Praise the Lord and pass the innovation!*

So, viewed in this heavenly light, maybe you'd agree with me that small business is our *single* best tool for combating climate change. The idea is not so preposterous after all, is it?

16

Yes, Maggie Thatcher, There is Such a Thing as Society

Margaret Thatcher (1925-2013), a conservative politician who was the first woman to serve as Prime Minister of Great Britain, was quotably plain-spoken. ("I don't mind how much my Ministers talk," she once remarked, "so long as they do what I say.") But certainly, the most famous (or infamous) words she ever uttered were in an interview she gave to *Woman's Own*, a British lifestyle magazine, in 1987. "There is no such thing as society," she declared.

Thatcher's comment soon went viral (or its equivalent back in those days). The British left, both appalled and delighted that she had so bluntly revealed her true and awful self, broadcast the quote far and wide. Whether she intended to or not, Maggie had thrown her enemies a big chunk of red meat.

For her enemies, here was proof — if anyone needed it — of the Prime Minister's callousness and cruelty. Here her worldview was made plain: a world wherein rampant individualism is exalted above all else; where no social rules or structure protect the weak from the predations of the powerful, the poor from the predations of the rich, and the unlucky from the predations of the lucky. My-oh-my-oh-my! Can anything be said in the old girl's defense?

Maybe we should look at what Thatcher said in context. Here's the full quote:

"I think we have gone through a period when too many children and people have been given to understand 'I have a problem, it is the Government's job to cope with it' … and so they are casting their problems upon society, and who is society? There are individual men and women and there are families, and no government can do anything except through people and people look to themselves first. It is our duty to look after ourselves and then after our neighbor … and people have got the entitlements too much in mind without the obligations."

A little further on, she repeated her point, using the exact words, "There is no such thing as society."

A politically neutral interpretation of Thatcher's statement in context might conclude she was asserting something reasonable: the primacy of individuals' responsibility for themselves, the primacy of families taking care of families, and the primacy of neighbors caring for neighbors. In fairness, these assertions are not the same thing as throwing the poor and disadvantaged to the wolves.

For myself — speaking as a *Small is Beautiful* freak — I can buy what the old girl said *up to a point*. If I could, I'd like to tell her this:

Look, Maggie, if you're talking about protecting the interests of individuals against those of the state, then I'm with you, heart and soul.

If you're talking about protecting the interests of local entities against those of centralized entities, I'm your boy.

If you're talking about protecting the interests of small entities against those of big entities, you can count on me.

But, sweetie, when right-wingers like you start talking like this, chills run up and down my spine. When you guys swoon over the hard work and thrift of small shopkeepers, somehow — in reality — it translates into *rampant hyper-individualism and leads to an economy dominated by rapacious wheeler-dealers.* Fess up, old girl, that's the England you created and that you left behind.

Geez Louise! Talk about perverted ideals!

Okay, I know you don't go about raving about the glories of hyper-individualism *as such*, but that's where your fine talk about homespun virtues leads! And it flies in the face of everything that *Edmund Burke* taught.

Look, I know that you once described Burke as "my ideological mentor." Well, he's *my* ideological mentor too. That makes us both *Burkeans.* We ought to be on the same page, dearie. But we sure as hell ain't!

I view your de facto embrace of hyper-individualism as anathema to the precepts of classic conservatism and, worse yet, as an affront to everything that Mother Nature teaches. Mag, where do you get off doing this? Whatever happened to the young girl who worked as a clerk in her father's grocery store?

Here's where you miss the boat, kiddo. There *is* such a thing as society — but it's not the government or the nation state. I'm talking about *society* as Burke defined it:

"Society is indeed a contract... [It is] a partnership not only between those who are living, but between those who are living, those who are dead, and those who are to be born."

Now, to me, Burke's statement is a version of the First Law of Ecology: *everything is connected to everything else.* To me, this natural connectedness is what constitutes the *true* human community, the *real* society to which we owe fealty and allegiance — Burke's "contract." This is how we humans are unified — perpetually and indissolubly.

This community is not remote, cold, and abstract like the state. It's not imposed on us through coercion. This community is intimate, warm, and as real as the DNA you inherited from your parents and that you bequeath to your children. This community is as comfy and cozy as a pair of old house shoes.

Tell me, sweetie, why do you right-wingers try so hard to deny or resist the pull of a community that embraces more than individuals, small groups, and localities? What is it that freaks you so? Is it a fear that your rights as an individual will be curtailed? Is it fear of state coercion?

Well, whatever your answer is, you've stumbled into gross hypocrisy. Your politics — unmasked — unleashes hyper-individualism into the world, and hyper-individualism is at war with the complex, interdependent webs that constitute humanity's true community.

Yes, the state is to be feared. And big, centralized institutions — public and private — are to be feared. But the web of ecology is to be loved, trusted, revered, and stoutly defended. Ecology is not socialism, Maggie, but it does compel an acknowledgement of our *interdependence*.

> *Take a look at what's going on in the world today. Everywhere you'll see democracy and the rule of law under savage assault by right-wing demagogues pulling every dirty trick in the book. And, mostly, the bastards getting away with it!*
>
> *Even the good old USA, the land of the brave and the home of the free, is not immune to this raging infection. Donald Trump, truculent and unruly, occupies the White House, pillaging and plundering that which he swore to preserve and protect. What a bad joke! Arguably, Trump is the single most imprudent man in America and, thus, a living, breathing rebuke of Edmund Burke, the founder of modern conservatism, who esteemed prudence above all other political virtues.*
>
> *Bad joke # 2: In a deal struck in hell, the nation's anti-evolutionists, climate change deniers, conspiracy theorists, faux populists, flat-earthers, homophobes, misogynists, racists, reactionaries, sanctimonious hypocrites, white supremacists, and xenophobes have teamed up with the nation's greedy phalanx of oligarchs and plutocrats to subvert the Republican Party and destroy everything good that it once stood for.*
>
> *Oh, what I'd give for a different politics! — The Author*

*"Edmund Burke, like all truly great men,
was both a conservative and a liberal."*

— Isaiah Berlin

17

Mother Nature's Politics:
She's Both a Conservative *and* a Liberal

It suits my purposes — and my fancy as well — to conceive of Mother Nature as a *politician,* to ascribe to her conscious aims and purposes that are *political.* Of course, my fancy won't suit everyone. The mere thought will probably drive academic ecologists around the bend. They are wary of ascribing any purpose to nature.

I, however, am neither an academic nor a scientist; I'm just a humble community organizer whose modest goal it is to make the world a better place. And to me, Mother Nature is one hell of a politician. If we humans had half a brain, we would follow her lead.

So, pursuing my fancy, I ask: what political cause would Mother Nature espouse? What would be her *program*? The answer leaps to mind in a word: *equilibrium.* Equilibrium describes a state in which opposing forces are *balanced.*

Of course, in politics, conservatism and liberalism are opposing forces. The conflict boils down to this (putting the best face on it): conservatives seek social *stability* while liberals seek social *change*. But today the idea that conservative and liberal politicians might get together and deliberately seek a balance between order and change is unthinkable. Our polarized politics rules it out.

Now, behold Mother Nature's balancing act! On the one hand, she works to impose and maintain order. On the other hand, she works to encourage and facilitate change. And this she accomplishes *simultaneously*. Here's the key: the balance she achieves is not static but *dynamic*.

Natural equilibrium is buffeted by constant *disturbances* that sometimes throw the balance off. These disturbances serve a purpose. They introduce change; they make room for something *new and different*. Typically, however, thanks to nature's vaunted resiliency, balance is restored after the effect of the disturbance is absorbed. Now, that's what I call *equilibrium*!

Okay, this brings us to this query: if equilibrium is the grand cause championed by Mother Nature, shouldn't it be the grand cause championed by *society*? One would think so, wouldn't one? Don't get your hopes up.

So how the heck does Mother Nature pull off her political gymnastics? To start with, she relies on *conservative methods* to work her will.

What Makes Mother Nature a Political Conservative?

Mother Nature strives to achieve equilibrium without reliance on the coercive power of the state. She steers clear of formal political processes: elections, government, laws, public policy, and government regulation. Instead, she favors:

- Social movements over political parties; cultural change over political change.

- Localism over centralism, she's a passionate promoter of local self-reliance and local production for local use.

- Organic change over central planning, change that bubbles from the bottom up over change that's imposed from the top down.

- Self-organizing systems over systems designed by humans.

- Webs over hierarchies, complexity over simplicity, and interdependence over independence.

- Countless uncoordinated acts by countless uncoordinated actors over coordinated efforts by teams of professional administrators, technicians, specialists, and experts.

- Leadership provided by entrepreneurs over leadership provided by politicians, the power of new tools to improve society over the power of new laws to do so.

Now, having described the methods used by Mother Nature as *conservative,* I must hasten to add that they are conservative in the classical, traditional sense. They are not the fraudulent, perverted version that passes for "conservatism" in today's debased political lexicon. (Donald Trump is the least conservative man in America.)

Mother Nature's conservative methods are the genuine article. They show up in the precepts laid down by Edmund Burke, the founder of modern conservatism. And the hallmark of his thinking is *stability through equilibrium.*

Mother Nature's Political Acolyte

Earlier in this book (Edmund Burke's Earth Day Speech), I argued that Burke, the founder of modern conservatism, derived his political ideas from his observations of nature.

For most of his career, Burke was a Whig reformer. (The Whigs were the liberals of the day. They staunchly opposed the concentration of power in the Crown.) As a Whig, Burke opposed slavery and most forms of capital punishment. He supported religious toleration and objected to the mistreatment of Catholics in Ireland. Appalled by conditions in the British Indian empire, Burke led a campaign to reform its administration and to protect the people of India from corruption and tyranny.

Burke detested injustice and the abuse of power. He supported the American revolution because it was fought in opposition to the arbitrary power by the King. But he opposed the French revolution because the mob's exercise of arbitrary power was destroying French culture and all the rich heritage of the past that it encompassed.

Edmund Burke was a conservative who believed, "Good order is the foundation of all things." But he was also a liberal who believed, "We must all obey the great law of change. It is the most powerful law of nature."

Burke urged change and progress. That makes him a liberal. But he urged change and progress *tempered by continuity and tradition.* That makes him a conservative.

Certainly, Burke cherished traditional values to the utmost, but — while the past was of great import — *a willingness to adapt to the inevitability of change would reaffirm traditional values under new circumstances.*

That's Burke's take on Mother Nature's equilibrium. What a team they make! And here's the lesson we can derive from their partnership. Isn't it clear that any leader astute enough to appreciate the world's boundless complexity must somehow embrace the best sentiments of both conservatism and liberalism? From this I conclude that — like Mother Nature and her star pupil, Edmund Burke — we should *all* be a conservative and a liberal.

What makes Mother Nature a liberal?

I can answer in a word: *diversity.*

No bleeding-heart liberal on earth cares more about diversity than Mother Nature does. She adores diversity and can't get enough of it. On this basis, I confidently argue that she's a committed liberal. Here's the great benefit of that. Mother Nature shows us how community unity can be achieved *while* embracing diversity in its myriad forms

All in all, Mother Nature's politics is a rebuke to humanity's shortcomings — to tribalism, racism, misogyny, homophobia, and humanity's disposition to fear and despise those who are different — "the other."

The Environmental Justice Movement

In this connection, it's necessary to acknowledge and honor the environmental justice movement.

Championed primarily by African Americans, Latinos, Asians and Pacific Islanders, and Native Americans, the environmental justice movement addresses a statistical fact: people who live, work and play in America's most polluted environments are commonly people of color and the poor.

Environmental justice advocates have shown that this is no accident. Communities of color, which are often poor, are routinely targeted to host facilities that have negative environmental impacts -- say, a landfill, dirty industrial plant or truck depot.

The statistics provide clear evidence of what the movement rightly calls "environmental racism." Communities of color have been battling this injustice for decades.

Mother Nature's Platform: Social Justice + Environmental Protection

Elsewhere in this book, I've argued that today's long overdue challenges to male dominance and white privilege are slowly being realized through *politics by other means.*

Now, let me grab this ball and run with it. I believe that the challenges to male dominance and white privilege being mounted by feminists and civil rights activists are likely *to benefit the environment enormously.*

I believe that a world where women exercise more power is likely to be more environmentally conscious and responsible. That's because women value *cooperation* more than men. Men value — and over-reward — *competition* and, doing so, have stressed natural systems to the breaking point. For example, women are much more likely than men to believe that climate change is for real and that humans are the cause of it.

I believe that a world that embraces social and racial diversity ardently is likely to be more environmentally conscious and responsible. That's because all the world's magnificent diversity — natural, cultural, social, ethnic, and sexual — flows from the generous bosom of Mother Nature. In this sense, all those who find reason to advocate and promote diversity are playing on the same team.

Rewilding vast portions of the earth may be the most direct, practical, economic, and efficient way we have to combat catastrophic climate change. That's because Mother Nature does almost all the work. And — glory be! — she works for free, and she works fast.

The aim of rewilding is to return the land to a wild state and to reintroduce the animals and plants that once thrived there. It's hard to overstate the ecological benefits. When habitats are restored and wildlife bounces back, vital ecological functions bounce back and on their own too. Voila! They are self-organizing!

Thanks to nature's magnificent resiliency, areas devastated by deforestation will soon reforest themselves. And these natural native forests require no maintenance. What's not to like? Thanks to Mother Nature, rewilding, once underway, is easier than falling off a log. — The Author

*I declare this world is so beautiful
that I can hardly believe it exists.*

— Emerson

18

Mother Nature's Got a Hold on You

Fortunately, we needn't tarry on our way to the crucial point of this essay. It's just a hop, skip, and jump away.

I needn't spend any time persuading you that Nature is the Great Healer. Hippocrates, the ultimate authority on the subject, completes the task in just seven words: "Nature itself is the best physician."

I needn't spend any time persuading you that Nature is the Great Teacher. All I need do is drag Einstein into the act: "Look deep into nature, and then you will understand everything better."

And why should I waste any breath persuading you that Nature is the Great Unifier when all I need do is quote Shakespeare's line? "One touch of nature makes the whole world kin."

Thanks, guys!

Now, what I do want to convince you of is this: Mother Nature is the Great Beauty.

This shouldn't be too hard either. Face it, we humans are all suckers for Mother Nature's beauty. She exercises a magnetic pull over each of us. Hell's bells, she's a sex symbol! If Mother Nature were a woman, she'd be Marilyn Monroe. (Hey, come to think of it, since it was Mother Nature who *created* Marilyn Monroe, my point is made.)

Here's where my chore gets a little harder. What I want to argue here is that Mother Nature's sex appeal can be used for political purposes, making the world a better place.

I contend that there's only one force on earth that's strong enough to counteract the tribalism and political polarization that's now disrupting the human community throughout the world. *That one thing is humanity's love of the wonder and beauty of nature.*

This is not baloney.

- Human beings are instinctively drawn to nature. Humans making this connection — directly experiencing nature's wonder and beauty — become healthier, stronger, wiser, and more compassionate.

- When humans connect with nature, they are enveloped in a sense of *community*. They feel *connected* to the rest of creation, to other people, to other life forms.

- This sense of *connectedness* can be used to overcome the fear and hatred of "the other" that foments continuous strife and violence in society.

If I'm right about this, then enabling people to directly experience nature — and *increasing* this experience — ought to be society's Number One Objective. But maybe I'm smoking dope. *Increasing* people's direct experience of nature is not on society's agenda. If anything, society is running *from* the direct experience of nature as if it were the plague. What gives?

Mother Nature's Downside

I'm a tree-hugger from way back. I conceive of the earth as a good mother who nurtures and supports us, who teaches and inspires us, and who keeps prodding us to do better. But this doesn't mean I'm oblivious to Mother Nature's downside. I shouldn't be talking behind her back, but the truth is the old girl can be a bitch on wheels. If you don't believe me, ask your prehistoric ancestors.

Our distant forbearers inhabited the wild for eons, and the rise of civilization may be seen as a flight from the wild's perils, insecurities, and uncertainties. Our plucky progenitors couldn't get out of the wild fast enough. Why should we, their descendants and heirs, now *go back in*?

It's not as if Mother Nature is going easy on us. Consider the many droughts, earthquakes, floods, hurricanes, tsunamis, and volcanic eruptions the old girl has inflicted — is *inflicting* — on us. Mother Nature can be savage and fearsome.

Now, — watch me! — I'm letting go of the tree I've been hugging this whole time. (*Whew!* It feels good! My arms are aching!) This separation from the object of my affections will allow me to do something I've been resisting, that is, to contemplate the dreadful possibility that maybe — just maybe

— Mother Nature doesn't have our best interests at heart. Indeed, her many critics claim she has no heart at all!

Furthermore, these critics claim that Mother Nature has no mind with which to conceive or pursue a *purpose*. To them, she is all erraticism and waywardness. To them, Mother Nature can be cruel and unrelenting, disrupting or taking lives, causing extinction, and messing up the economy. They point with pride to the walls of civilization that we've erected to protect us from her wayward vicissitudes.

Dare I — the tree-hugger — dissent?

Well, I *don't* dissent. I'm no Luddite who wants to turn the clock back to 1491. I readily concede the many benefits that industrial civilization delivers. I'm grateful my home is equipped with hot and cold running water, a furnace to warm me when it's cold, and an air conditioner to cool me when it's hot. And what would I do *—where would I go —* if I had no flush toilet? But, there's a downside to all these modern conveniences.

Civilization's Downside

So, civilization exists to protect us from Mother Nature's onslaughts. What else is new? But now, damnit, the shoe is on the other foot. We're subjected to *civilization's* onslaughts. Civilization weighs down on us. It's clamorous, congested, and confining. We're walled in by civilization, *literally.*

If, say, Mother Nature deposited a magnificent chunk of untamed wilderness right outside the Average Joe's front door, would the Average Joe bother to come out to explore it?

Probably not. The Average Joe is stuck inside the house where his face is glued to a TV, computer, smartphone, or tablet.

Whoa! "Deviation from nature," said Samuel Johnson, "is deviation from happiness." Let's get happy.

There are many pleasurable ways to experience nature that do your body and soul a world of good, and they vary boundlessly. You can go on solitary treks into the wilderness, or you can join a class doing yoga in an urban park. You can picnic in the country with your family and friends or sit alone in a garden, meditating. You can go bathing in the sunlight, or dancing in the moonlight. And on and on . . .

When all is said and done, what are we left with?

Hey, *look!* I've grabbed my tree again, and I'm hugging it as if my life depended on it (and maybe it *does* if the climate scientists are right). Here's where I take my stand. Screw the critics, I say! The beauty of nature is consistent and unrelenting. It's a beacon of light that is unwavering. We can count on it to guide us.

When we humans experience Mother Nature's wonder and beauty, we can't help being awed by her mystery, instructed by her functionality, and improved by her example.

This is good stuff. If human beings are going to clean up their act, we need more of it, lots more. And, thanks to Mother Nature's abundant generosity, there's a practical way to get what we need. It's called rewilding.

19

Rewilding: A Step Backwards into the Future

Many people — all of whom happen to be *homo sapiens* — are convinced that *homo sapiens* is the peak of evolution, its grandest accomplishment. Somehow the palpable vanity of this conviction escapes their notice, as has — dare I say? — the infinite mystery of the universe and the fact *homo sapiens* don't know diddly squat about it.

People who live in glass houses shouldn't throw stones. That includes me. What I believe is that the planet Earth — and all the marvels it contains — is the peak of evolution. God knows *I* can't imagine anything *grander*. Of course, I'm speaking here as an earthling; so, probably this is palpable vanity on my part.

In any case, the planet Earth and all it contains — including *homo sapiens* — is in great peril. We face the looming extinction of thousands of species, from lions and tigers and bears — *blah, blah, blah*. At the present rate, half of all species of plants and animals could disappear by the end of the century — *blah, blah, blah*. All this is a direct result of human depredations, habitat destruction, overpopulation, resource depletion, urban sprawl — *blah, blah, blah*.

Yeah, bet your ass, I'm as sick of these dreary recitations as you are. I want to put *blah, blah, blah* behind me. I want to step backwards into the future, and there's a process that allows me to do precisely that. It's called rewilding. (The term, *rewilding*, was coined by environmentalist Dave Foreman in the 1990s.)

In his book, *FERAL: Searching for Enchantment on the Frontiers of Rewilding*, environmental activist George Monbiot describes how the process works. "Rewilding, in my view, should involve reintroducing missing animals and plants, taking down the fences, blocking the drainage ditches, culling a few particularly invasive exotic species but otherwise standing back."

It's hard to overstate the ecological benefits of rewilding. The entire web of life is strengthened. When wildlife habitats are restored and biodiversity bounces back, vital ecological functions bounce back too. Functioning on their own, ecosystems prevent soil erosion and flooding. They purify water. They increase carbon storage. They adapt to climate change. Dear old Mother Nature works her tail off.

The Wolves in Yellowstone Park

One of the most celebrated examples of rewilding is the story of what happened when gray wolves were reintroduced to Yellowstone National Park in 1995. (The last wolf pack in the park had been hunted and killed in the 1920s, and the animals had been absent from there ever since.)

The wolves — iconic symbols of wildness — soon curbed explosive deer and elk populations that were stripping the landscape bare of vegetation. This helped bring back trees and shrubs. And birds of prey returned to feed on the increased carrion produced by wolf kills. Many other animals made a comeback, including beavers whose dam-building profoundly shapes the course of water flows in ecologically beneficial ways.

The wolves' return helped restore the park's riverbanks, which previously were stripped bare by over-browsing elk. And the return of plant life to the riverbanks stopped erosion. As a result, the flow of rivers then became less chaotic, forming pools of water that became inviting new habitats for wildlife.

Everything is connected to everything else, right? So, the reintroduction of wolves to Yellowstone — initially just 14 of them — eventually led to the restoration of the park's overall ecology. Mother Nature's bag of tricks is literally bottomless. You can't keep the old girl down.

Rewilding: What's Up for Grabs?

First, the bad news. Much of the planet's land surface has been deforested, burned, grazed, fertilized, and polluted. Vast tracts of this land are abandoned farms. In many places, farming has become unprofitable because the soil is exhausted. Besides, we are growing far more food on far less land. So, farming no longer keeps rural communities alive. Schools and businesses have shut down, and young people have fled to seek work in the city.

Here's the good news. These degraded landscapes, found in bits and pieces all over the globe, are prime candidates for rewilding. Potentially, this is a whopping big deal. These areas add up to 1.5 billion hectares, *an area equal to all of Russia.*

Here's the *really* good news. Lands that were once used for farms and logging are now becoming grasslands and forests *naturally*. Wildlife is returning there *naturally*.

For example, something like two thirds of the previously forested parts of the US are now reforesting *naturally* as farming and logging have retreated, especially in the northeast. Interestingly, this is happening in Russia too. After the fall of the Soviet Union, many of the state's collectivized farms were abandoned. They're rewilding too — *naturally.*

In France, rural abandonment has led to the restoration of forests, heathlands, and shrub-lands. In these areas, bears, wolves, and lynx are returning. So are vultures, ospreys, and other birds. Otters, beavers, fish are returning to the rivers. Loggerhead turtles are breeding again on the Mediterranean coast, and harbor seal populations are expanding.

This rewilding can be good news not just ecologically but economically. In the hills of southern Norway, for example, the natural reforestation of abandoned farmland is creating a newly diverse and enriched local economy. Nature's return has stimulated eco-tourism, hunting, fishing, outdoor education, snow sports, and hiking expeditions, creating many new local jobs.

Abandoned Dams

In past centuries, Americans seeking to build local industry with hydropower went on a dam-building spree. That spree has long since run its course. Hard to believe, but there are now approximately 26,000 dams in the States that are no longer of much or any use. Many have been abandoned and, like abandoned farms, these dam sites are prime candidates for rewilding.

For example, the Edwards Dam blocked the Kennebec River in Maine for 162 years. The dam destroyed wildlife and blocked the migration of salmon, shad, and herring, all prized by local commercial and recreational fishermen. But, as time went by, the dam provided only one-tenth of one percent of Maine's power supply.

Twenty years ago, the Edwards Dam was removed, and soon afterwards vegetation began to flourish and stabilize the riverbanks. Then fish reappeared — *swimming upstream* — just a few at first, then by the thousands and then by the millions. And what a profusion of fish it was: Atlantic sturgeons, sea lampreys, stripers, alewives, shad, blueback herring, and eels.

As the fish returned, the wildlife that feeds on aquatic life also returned — ospreys, bald eagles, black bears, minks, martins, and raccoons. The regional ecosystem has been strengthened by a river that is free to flow.

Today, the 17-acre riverfront site — formerly occupied by a textile mill and the dam — is a public park and the site of a summer carnival and a weekly farmers' market. There's also a canoe and kayak launch and a wooded riverfront nature trail. The community has fallen back in love with the river.

Happily, this story is typical. In the past 30 years, nearly 1,300 dams have been dismantled. And in 2017 alone, a record high of 87 dams were removed. Some of the biggest, most dramatic removals have been on the Elwha and White Salmon rivers in Washington, the Penobscot river in Maine, and the Eklutna River in Alaska.

Rewilding Around the World

All over the world, dozens of valiant efforts to rewild abandoned lands are being made by non-profit conservation organizations, both international and local.

Rewilding Europe, for example, a non-profit organization headquartered in the Netherlands, is working to create large, rewilded landscapes in at least ten different regions across Europe. They have sites in Bulgaria, Croatia, Germany, Italy, Poland, Portugal, Romania, Slovakia, Spain, and Sweden.

The Parque Patagonia in southern Chile

Parque Patagonia is an awe-inspiring example of rewilding on a grand scale. The site, once a 170,500-acre sheep ranch, was overgrazed to the point that native flora and fauna virtually disappeared including, most notably, the puma (known in North American as mountain lions).

More than 400 miles of fencing has been removed and the grasslands restored, allowing native wildlife to repopulate. The pumas have returned, their movement and behavior now monitored by GPS collars so park officials can better protect them.

The plan is to link Parque Patagonia to the nearby Jeinimeini and Tamango National Parks. This connection will create a nature preserve of 650,000 acres, an area large enough to allow wildlife populations to wander far and wide and to become self-sufficient.

Tourism into the parks has increased, benefiting the local economy. Many former ranch hands now work as park rangers.

A note on smaller efforts

In looking into the realms of rewilding, which I have spent some time doing the past couple of years, I discovered some more personal, individual efforts worth noting.

One is the work of Peter Allen and his wife Maureen on their small family farm nestled in the hills of the Driftless area outside of Viola, WI. The objective on Mastodon Valley Farm has been to restore the oak savanna that was the dominant ecosystem of the Midwest from Canada to Texas.

They raise cattle, pigs, sheep, goats, turkeys, and chickens that are rotated in sequences around the farm, mimicking patterns of grazing that might have been present among the Pleistocene megafauna (like Mastodons!). All animals have continuous access to sunshine and shade and are managed in ways that help restore functional ecosystems. Cattle are 100% ecosystem fed (grass, flowers, shrubs, and trees - not just grass!).

Grass, clover, flowers, chestnuts, hazelnuts, acorns, hickory nuts, mulberries, apples, cherries, and insects have proliferated on the land. The savanna's blend of nut-producing trees and grasslands was home to the most biodiversity of plants and animals of any biome in North America. It nourished the megafauna as well as us humans until modern history.

Another is the efforts by Isabella Tree and her husband Charlie Burrell to renew the ecosystem after decades of intensive agriculture on some 3,500 acres at Knepp Castle estate in West Sussex. I will not get into details of the project, which have been enjoyably described in a recent book by Isabella, *Wilding - the Return of Nature to a British Farm*.

The project, began in 2001 on land that had become economically unsustainable through years of intensive, industrialized farming practices, has become a glorious success. Their animals (Tamworth pigs, Exmoor ponies, Longhorn cows) live out in the open all year round and give birth unassisted by humans. Formerly common plants have returned in profusion, together with insects, bats, and other organisms. Scrubland, wetland, and other habitats are gradually rewiring themselves as herbicides and pesticides disappear. The increase in the variety and abundance of birds has been particularly astonishing.

I should also point out that both these projects are demonstrating the economic viability of returning the land to older realms of biodiversity. Our small farmers have a busy Community-supported agriculture business, supplying their local area with fresh produce and meat. The English estate also is producing agricultural goods for sale, and their safari centre has become a destination for wildlife tours and numerous specialist days for the general public to enjoy.

These are only two examples of efforts by other individuals. And they may not express it in quite this way, but I see that these true partnerships with Mother Nature may be the only path to saving the good life on our planet.

What the heck?! While we're at it, let's rewild half the earth!

Now, let's think big, *really big*. Let's think like Professor E. O. Wilson. In his book, *Half-Earth: Our Planet's Fight for Life*, the famous biologist and naturalist proposes to set aside half the Earth for the preservation of biodiversity.

This calls for the creation of huge parks to protect, restore and — most important — to *connect* habitats so animals can wander far and wide. Wilson claims that keeping these wilderness preserves free from human encroachment would stabilize more than 80 percent of the thousands of species now threatened with extinction.

This is not as impractical as it sounds. According to Wilson, habitats protected by governments *already* account for 15 percent of Earth's land area, That's not a bad start. Then he identifies some of the world's ecosystems that can still be reclaimed— the California redwood forests, the Amazon River basin, and the grasslands of the Serengeti. Then there's the Sahara Desert, Antarctica, Greenland, and Siberia. It adds up.

Pretty soon you're talking *continental scale.* And what have we got to lose, given that the extinction of our species is at stake. I say let's go for broke. Half the earth sounds about right to me, but then — as I've admitted — I'm a dedicated earthling and — obviously — as vain as a peacock.

Finally, there's this: when it comes to the task of actually rewilding the planet, Mother Nature is everything that *homo sapiens* are not. She's ready, willing, and able. She's tireless and resolute.

Of course, in this regard, I can't speak for all *homo sapiens,* only for myself. But I admit that, if it were up to me, I'd gladly hand the entire job over to dear old Mother Nature.

Then I'd scoot out of her way when she went to work. Content, I'd crawl in bed with a big bag of M&Ms and watch *Golden Girls* re-runs until the planet's glory was restored.

People create systems to advance their interests and to protect them from harm. But sometimes these systems take on a life of their own and, instead of serving people, systems betray them.

The true enemy of rewilding, as I see it, is the political/economic/industrial complex — "the system" — which is hellbent on the further destruction of nature and which appears impregnable and unstoppable.

This system, now thoroughly corrupt, is out of control and is playing by its own rules. It is unresponsive to the public. It evades any accountability to democracy or the rule of law.

The system suffers from gigantism and self-absorption to the point of blindness. It can neither learn nor change, so it is functionally stupid. It is headed for self-destruction and, when it goes, it will take us with it. That's the bad news.

Here's the good news. A big fast expanding crack has appeared in the edifice of this system. This crack is exposing the system's frailties, its internal contradictions, its hypocrisy, and its fraud.

Maybe the damned thing is not impregnable and unstoppable after all. — The Author

20

Conservatives ♥ Clean Energy

Liberals everywhere are enthusiastically advocating clean energy as a principal means of combatting climate change. That's no secret. What *is* secret — sort of — is that many conservatives are also enthusiastically advocating clean energy, but *not for the purpose of combatting climate change.* Heaven forbid! No way! Conservatives are advocating clean energy for *conservative* reasons. Just ask them.

"We come at this from a free-market point of view, a conservative point of view," says Scott Coenen, Executive Director of the Wisconsin Conservative Energy Forum, an organization formed just two years ago.

Conservatives claim that market forces, pure and simple, working on their own, have led them to this politically surprising embrace of what has long been a conspicuous liberal objective.

"Conservatives support renewable energy because it is clean and cheap," says Jared Noblitt, Executive Director of the Indiana Conservative Alliance for Energy. "Market forces are causing the cost of renewable energy options like utility-scale wind and solar to plummet — today making them the least expensive energy source in most cases."

Clean energy is economical. And what is economical serves the goal of *fiscal conservatism.* Clean energy enables homeowners, businesses, and schools to greatly reduce energy waste, thereby encouraging thrift and efficiency.

Conservatives favor more *competition* in energy markets. They love the increased freedom of choice that competition often provides, and they cherish the freedom to choose the source and type of energy they use.

For example, conservatives welcome the distributed generation of energy which enables consumers to generate their own energy on-site. Distributed generation employs small-scale technologies like solar panels on the rooftops of single-family homes. The is the very definition of *local self-reliance*, a hallmark of conservative philosophy.

Conservatives see clean energy as a powerful force for *economic growth*. Already, it has created thousands of *new jobs*, billions of dollars in investments (especially in the Sun Belt and Great Plains) and produced many new business and manufacturing opportunities.

Conservatives, who put *national security* interests at the top of their political agenda, point out that clean energy contributes mightily to the goal of *energy independence*. Specifically, in this connection, conservatives cite the resilience of clean energy to terrorist strikes. They argue, persuasively, that solar panels and wind turbines are far less vulnerable to attack than are big, centralized power plants.

In short, conservatives claim that clean energy and conservative values go together, like love and marriage. I couldn't agree more! I think it's a marriage made in heaven.

(Perhaps I should make myself crystal clear here. The principles I'm talking about are those propounded by Edmund Burke, the founder of modern conservatism. I am definitely not talking about anything whatever to do with the tweets, rants, lies, and conspiracy theories of Donald Trump, a faux conservative if ever there was one. His "conservatism" is nothing but a rip-off and a racket, and honest conservatives know it.)

Red States & Green Power

The growing support of conservatives in red states for clean energy should come as no surprise. It just so happens that most of the states that are sunny, *naturally*, are red, *politically*. Here they are: Alaska, Alabama, Florida, Idaho, Kansas, Montana, Nebraska, North Dakota, Oklahoma, South Dakota, Texas, Wyoming, and Utah.

Similarly, it just so happens that most of the states that are windy, *naturally*, are red, *politically*. Here they are: Iowa, Kansas, Montana, Nebraska, North Dakota, Oklahoma, South Dakota, Texas, Wyoming, and Utah.

Here's how this is playing out among the states:

- Wyoming leads the country in increasing its renewable energy capacity overall.

- Kansas ranks first amongst the states for increasing its share of renewable energy in electricity (it tripled its wind power in four years).

- North Dakota leads the states in terms of wind energy per capita.

- Nevada boasts more solar power per capita than anywhere in the country.

- North Carolina is now the nation's second largest solar market (after California).

- In the past year, Utah, North Carolina, and Texas each installed more than 1 gigawatt of solar, or enough to power about 700,000 homes.

- Iowa now obtains nearly a third of its power from solar energy.

- Texas is harnessing its great wind generation potential. Today, more of the state's electricity comes from wind than coal.

- Wind energy now provides more than 30% of the electricity supply in Iowa, Kansas, Oklahoma, and South Dakota.

Conservative values = a new conservative social movement

Lo and behold, a conservative political movement on behalf of clean energy has formed around the country. This movement has erupted everywhere, but — get this— *it is strongest in red states.* Here's evidence of it:

- Conservatives for Clean Energy (Florida)
- Conservatives for Clean Energy (Georgia)
- Indiana Conservative Alliance for Energy
- Iowa Conservative Energy Forum
- Kansans for Wind Energy

- Conservatives for Clean Energy (North Carolina)
- Ohio Conservative Energy Forum
- Conservatives for Clean Energy (South Carolina)
- Conservative Texans for Energy Innovation
- Conservatives for Clean Energy (Virginia)

Red States + Green Power = A New Politics?

Here's an eye-opener. Take a look at what these various opinion polls reveal about the affinity of conservative voters for clean energy.

According to the Conservative Energy Network, a significant majority of US voters (81%) across all party affiliations said they would vote for elected officials who support clean energy development such as wind and solar.

A poll taken by the Indiana Conservative Alliance for Energy indicates that conservatives in Indiana support solar development 71% to 24% and wind development by a margin of 57% to 38%. The poll also found that 57% of Republicans are more likely to support a candidate for elected office who favors increasing the use of renewable energy.

In Florida, 82% of the conservatives polled support action to accelerate the development and use of clean energy in the state. And a majority declared that they are more likely to vote for a candidate who supports the development of clean energy.

Similarly, a poll released by the Ohio Conservative Energy Forum says more than two-thirds of conservative respondents support renewable energy development.

An August 2018 survey in Iowa found that 78% of the state's conservatives believe their government should pursue an energy strategy of lowering dependence on fossil fuels and allowing an increase in electric generation from emerging technologies like renewable energy as well as more energy efficiency.

The Wind Coalition and the Climate and Energy Project in Kansas released poll data showing that Kansans overwhelmingly support the development of renewable energy resources in Kansas, with 73% of Republicans supporting a state renewable energy law.

Conservatives for Clean Energy (South Carolina) released a new poll in March 2019 showing strong support for development of clean energy in the state, with 72% of South Carolina self-identified conservatives weighing in with that support.

In March 2019, the Conservative Texans for Energy Innovation released a poll in which Republican and Independent voters across the state expressed a belief that more use of clean energy will:

- Help the economy and create jobs (63%)
- Improve reliability of the electric grid (63%)
- Increase customer choice (75%)
- Help Texas continue to lead the nation in energy technology (79%)
- Result in more energy innovation (81%)

A survey in Virginia found 80% of respondents in support of taking action to accelerate the development and use of clean energy in the state, with 79% of those identified as Somewhat Conservative and 58% of those Very Conservative agreeing. Voters across party lines said they are more likely to vote for a candidate who supports the development of clean energy, with more than 55% of Republicans responding thus.

Is this a crack I see before me?

As we've seen, some of the fastest progress on clean energy is occurring in states led by Republican governors and legislators, and in states carried by Donald Trump in the 2016 presidential election.

Ponder this: the five states that get the largest share of their power from wind — Texas, Iowa, Kansas, Oklahoma, and South Dakota — are all led by Republicans and went for Donald Trump in the 2016 presidential election.

Now, we know that the Trump administration and Republicans in Congress are aggressively anti-clean energy. In these circles, it's the fossil fuel boys who call the shots. Doesn't all the evidence of grassroots conservative support for clean energy that I've provided here expose a major conflict among conservatives?

I predict a scrap breaking out between pro-fossil fuel/pro-utility Republican elites and pro-renewable grassroots conservatives. Already, many local policy fights have pitted grassroots conservative activists against well-funded, right-wing advocacy groups aligned with fossil fuel producers and power utilities.

How will all this play out in 2020? The fossil fuel boys are accustomed to calling the shots when it comes to the politics of energy, and they blandly assume that grassroots political conservatives are safely and permanently in their pockets. Next time, they may find their pockets empty.

*The individual is foolish;
the multitude, for the moment is foolish,
when they act without deliberation;
but the species is wise, and, when time is given to it,
as a species it always acts right.*

— Edmund Burke

21

We Can Learn, We Can Change, We Can Grow

The story of the environmental revolution, as recounted in this book, describes an astonishing leap forward in social learning, as great as any in human history. Here is proof aplenty that people can indeed *learn, change, and grow*. Let us rejoice in this. We've got a hell of a lot going for us.

To recap, here are the jewels in the environmental crown:

- The political legacy, a raft of basic environmental protection statutes that remain the law of the land to this day;

- The countless new green businesses and industries that are engulfing the old industrial economy, the countless new green technology innovations that are being unleashed into the world by green tinkerers and entrepreneurs, and the countless new clean and green jobs that have been produced in the process;

- The many forms of social organization that have been greened up the wazoo: education and academe, the professions, commerce, science, the arts and humanities, and the burgeoning pop culture.

- The greening of the cultural and social values of Generations X, Y, and Z and the revolutionary impacts of these changes — transforming politics, the economy, and society as a whole for the better.

Then there's this: the environmental revolution's *politicalization of the ecological worldview.*

The First Law of Ecology — everything is connected to everything else — declares that there are no hierarchies in nature, no ruling classes, no elites, no superiority of one thing over another. Natural systems consist of complex, interdependent webs in which all components are equally important.

So it is, I argue, that the First Law of Ecology *mandates social justice.* In this regard, its *political* significance cannot be overestimated.

- The First Law of Ecology is a Magna Carta for the soil and the land, for trees and forests, for lakes and rivers, and for seas and oceans.

- It's a Declaration of Independence for animals. They too have a right to life, liberty, and the pursuit of happiness.

- It's an Emancipation Proclamation for all the diversity — social, cultural, ethnic, racial, and sexual as well as natural — being subjugated by an obsolete patriarchal culture that draws its strength from the imposition of mindless uniformity.

"Wow" is all I can say!

I must confess that revisiting this list fills me with pride. What impressive accomplishments — a brief historical era in which one big wave of constructive social change followed another! To be honest, I'd be rubbing my eyes in disbelief if I hadn't been an active participant in the whole thing from the very beginning. Just look at me! I'm actually exhausted from patting myself on the back. *Ouch!* I think I've just pulled my shoulder out of its socket!

But my cup of exuberance runneth over. I'm duty bound to express thanks to the countless *other people* who fought on the side of the environmental revolution and who bagged all these victories. In fact, from the bottom of my heart, I offer thanks to anyone and everyone who had even the slightest thing to do with these accomplishments. Oh, what the heck! *Why hold back?!* I congratulate all *humanity* on its boundless capacity for learning, for changing, and growing. You are one hell of a great species!

There's only one catch. *What if none of this makes any difference?!*

Is it enough? Will it happen in time?

Okay, even with all this great stuff going for us, we must ask, is it going to be *enough* to prevent catastrophic climate change? I sure hope so, but I don't know for sure. *Nobody knows for sure!*

And what if all this good stuff kicks in, but it's *too late* to prevent the catastrophe overtaking us? Scientists claim we've only got a few years to make drastic changes in society's operations. Can society change that much, that fast?

Once again, I certainly hope so, but I don't know for sure. *Nobody knows for sure!*

A Nip-and-Tuck Situation

At the start of this book, I laid my cards on the table. My basic assumption, I declared, was that *what we've got here is a nip-and-tuck situation.*

Nip-and-tuck means that the outcome of a conflict is too close to call. It means that the forces arrayed on either side of a conflict are — at present, anyway — too evenly matched to ensure victory for one side or the other.

As I see it, that's the case here. On the one hand, we have the legacy of the environmental revolution, a mighty force indeed, as I have labored to show. On the other hand, we have the opposing force of climate change, measured and calculated by the world's scientists, revealing it to be a force at least equal to the environmental revolution. Where must one come out?

Now, at the end of this book, after busting my ass toiling over these questions, I'm sticking to my guns. When all is said and done, I continue to maintain *what we've got here is a nip-and-tuck situation.* And that means we've got a chance.

Let's seize this chance with all our might. And let's start by taking back control of our political system.

It's the Demographics, Stupid!

The youngest Americans — millennials and Generation Z — are set to exercise their political muscle in 2020, making up 37% of the electorate, according to Pew Research. This matters a lot. Younger generations are by far more racially and ethnically diverse than old farts are.

Generation Z will be voting for the first time. They will represent one in ten voters. These youngest Americans have continued and deepened many of the political trends favored by millennials. Both tend to be more liberal than older generations, and — in particular — both tend to believe that the earth is getting warmer due to human activity.

Based on these demographics, I'm hoping that voters in 2020 will unite to throw the climate-denying rascals out, and thus restore the vitality, accountability, and responsiveness of the American political system. (Among the many benefits to follow is one that affects me personally: I can then die happy.)

Plus, I've got this hope to cling to: if the climate-denying rascals don't get thrown out in 2020, *they most assuredly will be in 2024.* That's how the demographic cookie is crumbling.

Demographically speaking, there are good times just around the corner.

Now, to wrap this book up — finally — once and for all — I feel obliged to exit the stage with a rhetorical flourish worthy of the historical moment we inhabit and the fast approaching crisis we face. For this purpose, I can do no better than to steal a passage from Winston Churchill who inhabited a similar moment and who faced a similar crisis.

Here goes:

We shall green the rooftops, we shall green the buildings, the streets, and roadways; we shall cleanse with growing confidence and growing strength the air and the water.

We shall defend our planet, whatever the cost may be.

We shall rewild the beaches, we shall rewild the countryside; we shall rewild the fields and the forests; we shall rewild the hills; we shall never stop rewilding.

Let us therefore brace ourselves to our duties and so bear ourselves that, if the human species and its civilization last for a million years, people will still say, "This was their greenest hour."

Epilogue

In these pages, I've made extraordinary and audacious claims on behalf of the environmental revolution. Its consequences, I claim, are constructive, benevolent, omnipresent, and — going for the gold — *transformative*, changing world history for the better.

World revolutions on this scale are few and far between. Here's how I encapsulate history: the agricultural revolution made civilization possible, the scientific revolution made civilization better, the industrial revolution made civilization untenable, and the — still unfolding — environmental revolution makes civilization possible *anew*.

Mind you, I'm not claiming everything is hunky-dory. It most certainly is not. Just keeping up with the statistics about the changing climate can induce suicidal thoughts. And this catastrophe is occurring at a time when democratic governance and the rule of law are under savage attack everywhere you look. (*Stop the world, my soul cries out, I want to get off!*)

All I can say is — hallelujah! — there's more than one way to skin a cat! I've striven in this book to show *this other way*. And I've done so to my satisfaction, and I hope to the reader's as well. (My apologies to People for the Ethical Treatment of Animals, and my assurances that no cats were skinned in the production of this book.)

Cultural and social values are more important than politics

Thanks to the environmental revolution, society has been outfitted with a new set of cultural and social values. These values are consistent with *the ecological worldview,* which — while turning the old man-centered universe inside out — actually corrected our comprehension of the world around us. The ecological worldview:

- Restored natural creation to its rightful place — front and center — in how we view life and human existence; and

- Restored humanity to its rightful place — not at the pinnacle of an evolutionary pyramid — but a species ensconced with countless others in the supportive, protective, complex, interdependent, and resilient webs that comprise natural creation.

This is a big friggin' deal, maybe the *biggest* of all deals. That's because culture is more determinative of how we behave than *politics* is. I conclude — that if the massive conflict over environmental protection is a culture war — *then environmentalists have won it.*

(Bear in mind that we're still in the *midst* of the environmental revolution. There are more consequences yet to come. The reader is advised to hang on to his or her hat.)

The entire apparatus of civilization has been upgraded

The environmental revolution has equipped society with new knowledge, new skills, and new tools, an *upgrade* of civilization.

This is another big friggin' deal. Repeatedly, I've asserted that — thanks to the environmental revolution — *we know what to do, and we know how to do it.*

Once again — to make my point — I invoke the splendid example of green buildings which, as I see things, are extraordinary manifestations of human genius, right up there with Renaissance art, Mozart's music, and Einstein's theories. If the species survives, I'll bet that future generations will look back on the achievements of today's green architects and builders with awe and gratitude.

Green buildings are masterpieces of ecological design. They don't consume energy; they *produce* it. These buildings don't waste water; they *conserve* it. They don't increase greenhouse gas emissions — they *reduce* them. And they're beautiful too! Elegant! Today, every new structure being built should be *green,* or it shouldn't be built at all.

The use of conservative methods to pursue radical ecological goals

The environmental revolution has promulgated a set of grand and glorious goals, especially these:

- The transformation of the industrial economy into ecological sustainability;

- The reduction of greenhouse gas emissions to a bare minimum;

- The rewilding of vast portions of the damaged earth;

- The establishment of environmental justice to ensure that environmental protection includes protection of disadvantaged people on whom the worst pollution is routinely dumped;

- The embrace by society of diversity — in all its varied forms — as the foundation of social justice, with liberty and equality for all.

In these pages, I've described how the pursuit of these *radical* goals has relied on methods that are *conservative*. And here I mean conservative in the *classic* sense — meaning that they're among the philosophical approaches championed by Edmund Burke, the founder of modern conservatism (and grotesquely mutilated by Donald Trump, the destroyer of modern conservatism.)

Here are three such methods:

1. Social movements succeed through *organic change* — not through top-down, command and control approaches. By definition, organic change — small-scale, incremental, decentralized, emanating from the bottom up — is a conservative method, and moreover, it's Mother Nature's preferred mode of operation.

2. All over the world, tinkerers and entrepreneurs are devising technological innovations that are, bit by bit, compelling the giants of the old industrial order to embrace sustainability *or die.* (Prime example: the electric industry.) This transition is being achieved

through the process of *creative destruction*, yet another conservative method of social change.

Bear in mind that these new technologies win out not merely because they are environmentally benign, but because they are superior to the old technologies they displace in every way: more productive, economical, efficient, reliable, and resilient.

3. Social change is often secured through the medium of *countless acts by countless actors.* Social change secured in this manner possesses a *legitimacy* that nothing else does because it emanates from within the community and, hence, is a *genuine* expression of community values. And this too is another conservative method championed by Edmund Burke.

Social change secured in this manner is hard to resist or to combat. It treads on little cat feet. What a fabulous prescription for social change!

For example, when millions of consumers worldwide decide — *on their own* (as they have) — to stop eating meat or to greatly reduce their meat consumption, it's an act of great consequence and not just economically. Bear in mind that many of these people have cut back on meat consumption as a deliberate *political* act. What are meat producers to do? Get a compliant and corrupt Congress to pass a law *compelling* us to eat meat?

And lest we forget: the astonishing success of Earth Day in 1970 was achieved through the medium of countless acts by countless actors.

Twenty-five million people all over the country turned out to do *their own thing* — whatever it was, wherever they were. That's the *only way* Earth Day could have succeeded. Again, I declare nobody organized Earth Day; *Earth Day organized itself.*

The political plusses of using conservative methods to pursue radical ecological goals

Conservative methods of social change are subtle. They operate in the shadows. These qualities enable environmentalists to play *politics by other means,* which relies on stealth and surprise to succeed. Oh, what fun!

Politics by other means avoids direct confrontation or conflict with the powerful, entrenched opposition. For instance, it doesn't focus on winning elections or getting a bill passed by Congress. Instead, politics by other means tunnels beneath the opposition; it runs rings around it or flies over its head. Result: the entrenched opposition is confounded.

Take same sex marriage, for example. When its advocates ran into a solid wall of political opposition, they turned to pop culture for support. And guess what, pop culture came through! (Some social critics now claim that — these days — pop culture is more powerful than politics.)

Advocates of same sex marriage argued their case through the medium of television sit-coms, and public opinion shifted in their direction. They won! Opponents of same sex marriage are still scratching their heads, trying to figure out what the hell happened to them.

Besides confounding the opposition, playing politics by other means has another notable strategic advantage. By avoiding direct engagement with the enemy, it obviates the interminable partisan and ideological feuding over just *how* to protect the environment. It dispenses with the blather. It sneaks in through the back door, operates on the sly, and gets the job done.

Above, I proclaimed environmentalists the victor of the culture war over environmental protection. I think we should take great comfort and pride in this victory. And I think we should acknowledge — at least to ourselves — that this victory was gained through the use of *conservative methods*. We should confidently continue our trek, picking our way carefully down this hidden, rocky, and crooked path. Sneaking around is good for the environment.

But what about *the political war*, where all the news from the front seems to be bad? Here, I think, we must take a longish view. Here's what I see.

I believe that "politics by other means" can ultimately lead us to conventional political victories, even to the restoration of the integrity of the political system, a goal devoutly to be desired. That's because politics by other means steadily undermines the defensive structure of the opposition, however entrenched and impregnable it appears. Ultimately the weakened structure is easy to push over. Sometimes it falls of its own accord.

The demographic times, they are a-changin'

A bit earlier I stated that changes in cultural and social values are *more important* than political changes, observing what a big deal this was.

Well, here's where the deal gets even *bigger*: when it comes to the *political* manifestation of these new cultural and social values, you ain't seen nuthin' yet. Today's youth are people from the future.

Let's take a look backwards: if someone had told me on Earth Day in 1970 that the most profound consequence of the event would be that it changed the cultural and social values *of generations yet unborn*, I would have laughed in his face. But — great jumping Jehosephat! — that's what happened!

Subsequently, each new generation post-Earth Day — Generations X, Y, and Z, as they are known — has emerged more strongly committed to environmental protection than the generation preceding it. Here's who these people are:

- Generation X follows the baby boomers and precedes the millennials. It consists of people born between the mid-60s to the early 80s;

- Generation Y consists of people born between the 1980's and the year 2000 — they're the Millennials;

- Generation Z consists of people born since 2000.

Ponder this: Millennials and members of Generation Z strongly agree that climate change is the biggest problem they face. They've had it up to here with climate denial.

And ponder this: Millennials and Generation Z will make up 37% of the electorate in 2020. That percentage will, of course, be even larger when 2024 rolls around.

It's my confident hope that these demographic changes will bring about the political destruction of climate denial and the political defeat of the fossil fuel boys.

Here's the equation that dances around inside my brain. The environmental revolution = changes in cultural and social values + the rise of Generations X, Y, and Z = the coming second triumph of environmentalism.

And so — grinning like a Cheshire cat — I close this account confident that the off-beat contentions I've been making throughout this book have been established once and for all. Yes, by golly, I've done what I set out to do. I've explained *how history is actually changed for the better!*

I assume the Nobel Prize committee has my contact information.

145

About the Author

In the 1960s, working as a community organizer for the Conservation Foundation, Byron Kennard travelled the country helping to form local civic organizations to combat environmental pollution. For this work, he was awarded the Leadership Medal of the United Nations Environment Program for "distinguished contribution to the cause of the environment."

Kennard's community organizing helped form the national environmental movement and also helped lay the groundwork for the explosion of civic and political action on Earth Day in 1970. In the following decades, he served in many environmental posts, including that of National Chair of Earth Day '80.

A longtime "small is beautiful," devotee, Kennard founded the Center for Small Business and the Environment in 1998 to promote the idea that small green entrepreneurial businesses are the key to environmental protection and thus, as well, the key to combating climate change. Kennard served as CSBE's Executive Director until 2012.

Kennard is the author of *Nothing Can Be Done, Everything Is Possible*, which the Christian Science Monitor called "a primer for the modern-day activist."

Photograph by Vivian Spiegelman

Kennard has been a longtime contributor to the Huffington Post where his blogs appeared on *HuffPost Green*, *HuffPost Comedy*, and *HuffPost Gay Voices*. You can see these at *huffpost.com/author/byron-kennard.*

See also Byron Kennard's Capers at *byronkennard.com.*

Acknowledgements

If I do say so myself, when it comes to working with other people, I'm pretty darned good at it. Any community organizer worth his salt has to be. That is to say, I've succeeded in dragging a bunch of other people into my act and getting them to work for me as unpaid volunteers. (Now, that's what I call *community organizing*.)

But, seriously, folks — this little book is the result of considerable exertion, not just mine, but of others as well. I freely acknowledge this debt. Giving credit where credit is due is second nature to me. That's how — in the course of my long and checkered career — I managed to make the world a better place.

I must start with crediting Glenn David Pinder, my lover, soulmate, and creative partner for fifty-five years *and* my legally wed spouse for the last five. Glenn is a superb copyeditor. He looks askance at every word I write, turning it inside out to make sure it's *the right word*. A word that is only the *almost right word* gets the heave-ho. A champion nitpicker, Glenn has never allowed a misplaced comma to survive for long in all my voluminous scribblings. Around him, semi-colons snap to attention and line up to do their duty, nothing more and nothing less.

Next up are Gordon Binder and Michael Rawson, our best friends for decades. I don't make a move without Gordon's shrewd political advice. He delights in curbing all the excesses in which I take delight, ideological as well as literary. Gordon is habitually cautious, and I am habitually audacious (although you wouldn't know it from the looks of me). In life, caution is called for more often than is audacity. On the other hand, Michael, Gordon's spouse — who *is* a caution — pays me the great compliment of understanding what I'm saying better than I do. He's worth his weight in gold. He's continually telling me how good I am.

Thirdly, there's the incomparable Joe Handy, a dreamboat of a collaborator if ever there was one. Joe designed this book and oversaw its production, with help and advice from his estimable spouse, Mark Crosby. I'm absolutely mad about everything they did. Joe is also a publicist and promoter extraordinaire. If anybody can put me on the map, he can. (I'm ready for my close-up, Mr. Handy.)

Next, I wish to thank Peter Harnik for his help. Peter was the last reviewer to read the entire manuscript, and his enthusiastic sign-off on the final draft signaled for me a welcome end to a prolonged writing chore. Though a cherished friend, Peter has no compunction about wrestling me to the mat when we disagree about something. That's all to the good. When we're done fighting the draft has always benefited.

Hail, hail, the gang's all here!

I'm grateful to the friends and collaborators who read portions of the draft manuscript and generously provided me with "blurbs" for promotional purposes. They are George Alderson, Barbara Reid Alexander, Carl Sferrazza Anthony, Gordon Binder, Brock Evans, Hazel Henderson, Jamie Kirchick,

Catherine Lerza, Sam Love, Amory Lovins, Mike McCabe, Carl Pope, Peter H. Schuck, and Scott Sklar.

The fulsomeness of their praise would probably cause most people to blush in embarrassment, but somehow, I manage to take it as my due. If any of these sweetie-pies ever ask me to return the favor, my eloquence will flow like the fountains of Rome, I promise.

Other friends who read portions of the book in progress and provided helpful comments include Joan Martin Brown, Jeff Church, Mark Crosby, Ed Farha, Sharon Francis, David Frenkil, Sarah Marshall, Rich Tafel, and Chris Wingert. (I apologize if I've left someone out who should be included.)

For advice on the cover art design, I'm grateful to Martin Tarratt and Langley Spurlock, two highly accomplished artists who are old, dear friends. In this connection, I'm obliged to thank (once again) Gordon Binder and Michael Rawson — both accomplished artists too.

In addition. I wish to thank Ben Weinberg who produced a promotional video for the book, and did his usual bang-up job. He's a pleasure to work with.

Unavoidable conclusion: reviewing this lengthy list of all the brainy and talented people who've helped me, I'm surprised that this book didn't write itself!

Alas, it did not.

Burkeans in my Midst

One might think my open admiration for Edmund Burke and the classic concepts of conservatism he proclaimed would land me in hot water with my natural constituency, the environmentalists, most of whom are red-hot liberals. Well, it hasn't. Not so far, anyway.

There's an explanation for this. My argument for Burkean environmentalism has simply been *ignored* by liberal environmentalists. It hasn't been rejected because it hasn't been heard. What *did* happen, as I see it, was that *cognitive dissonance* kicked in.

Cognitive dissonance is a mental conflict that occurs when people hold contradictory beliefs, ideas, or values, and the resultant stress causes their minds to go blank. Consider this:

• On the one hand, liberals are *environmentalists*. This commits them to the ecological worldview — that is, to faith in organic change and reliance on incremental, small-scale, decentralized processes, all guided by the exercise of prudent restraint.

• On the other hand, environmentalists are *liberals*. This commits them to social reform through mobilization of the collective will — that is, through central planning, command and control approaches, and reliance on public law and government regulation, all guided by a certainty about prospects for fundamental systemic change.

Clearly, these commitments are incompatible. So advocating Burkean environmentalism is hard going when the minds of those in your intended audience go blank at the very mention of the idea. Fortunately, in this advocacy, I've had support and encouragement from three prominent conservative intellectuals who are also dear friends. They are:

• Jamie Kirchick, a visiting fellow at the Brookings Institution, and a highly regarded conservative reporter and foreign correspondent. Jamie is the author of *The End of Europe: Dictators, Demagogues, and the Coming Dark Age* (Yale, 2017). Jamie also writes frequently about American gay politics and international gay rights. He is a recipient of the National Lesbian and Gay Journalists Association Journalist of the Year Award. Currently he is at work on a history of gay Washington, DC.

• Peter H. Schuck, an emeritus professor at Yale Law School, is the author most recently of *One Nation Undecided: Clear Thinking About Five Hard Issues That Divide Us*. Peter and I go way back. I've learned a lot from his conservative take on things. I remember being jolted by an op-ed he wrote for the *New York Times* in 1981 (One of a great many he's written over the years.) He described what he perceived as a major contradiction in the attitude and values of liberals in their divergent approaches to environmental protection and social reform. *Yes!* Peter identified the very cognitive hangup I've just described in the passage above. Imagine, he was prescient about this back then. I'm sorry to say that Peter's prescience hasn't served to remove the partisan and ideological blinders that still — 40 years later — impair the vision of most liberal environmentalists, and that prevents them from seeing the applicability of conservative methods to ecological goals.

• Rich Tafel is the President of Public Squared, a social change strategy company. Tafel, who is ordained, is the minister at the Church of the Holy City in Washington DC. (He officiated at my wedding to Glenn Pinder five years ago.) In 1993, Rich founded Log Cabin Republicans in an effort to bridge the gap between the conservative and gay community in America. He is the author of *Party Crasher: A Gay Republican Challenges Politics as Usual* (Simon & Schuster).

Here, I'm also obliged to mention the support and encouragement for Burkean environmentalism I've received from prominent conservatives who are neither friends, nor colleagues, but who read my essay, *Edmund Burke's Earth Day Speech*, and who were kind enough to send me messages praising it. They are:

• Yuval Levin, founding editor of National Affairs; author of *The Great Debate: Edmund Burke, Thomas Paine, and the Birth of Right and Left*

• Sir Roger Scruton, author of *Green Conservatism: How to Think Seriously About the Planet: The Case for an Environmental Conservatism (Oxford University Press)*

• Jerry Taylor, President, The Niskanen Center, a libertarian think tank, and author of *The Conservative Case for a Carbon Tax.*

In this connection, I also received glad tidings from Carl T. Bogus, a professor at the Roger Williams University School of Law. Professor Bogus is a liberal who writes wonderfully well about conservatism, mixing admiration with critique. He is the author of *William F. Buckley Jr. and the Rise of American Conservatism.*

Perhaps this book will rattle the minds of liberal environmentalists, opening them up to a consideration of Burkean environmentalism and its political appeal. As I see things, it's an idea whose time has come.

Small Business is Beautiful

In dedicating this book to Fritz Schumacher, I acknowledged my immense debt to him. *Small is Beautiful* has been my political Bible since 1973. The importance of *scale* as a factor in all human endeavors has permeated my thinking about society, politics, the economy, and most everything ever since. Eventually, this outlook led me to found the Center for Small Business and the Environment in 1995 and to serve as its Executive Director for seventeen years until my retirement in 2012.

This project was based on the premise that small green businesses and green entrepreneurs are the best tools we have to transform the industrial economy into ecological sustainability — and thus the best tools we have to actually protect and restore the environment.

Dear me, this premise turned out to be another hard row to hoe!

I'm sorry to report that most liberals and environmentalists do not view small business with the respect and admiration that I do. Small business is, after all, *small*, and environmental problems are *big*. What's the connection?

Liberals, as previously noted, are centralists in outlook, and centralists are devotees of *quantification*. If something can't be counted, measured, segmented and evaluated on its own, it doesn't exist. So, what do centralists make of "countless acts by countless actors?" *Nothing* is the answer.

So here again my message is met with indifference by liberal environmentalists, my old pals. and my intended audience. But, thank goodness, here again I found a new band of faithful friends and allies. People in the small business community got my message right off the bat! They needn't need to be convinced that small business is a wondrous tool for protecting and restoring the environment. Why not? Small business can do anything.

What wonderful allies small business people make!

My first small business ally was Helen Anderson, a California small business owner who was then a Board Member of the National Small Business Association. Helen became my guide and sponsor in the small business community. I am grateful to her still.

Thanks to Helen, I got a lot of help and support from the National Small Business Association (NSBA), the nation's oldest small business advocacy organization, and a trusted voice in the community. I owe thanks to Todd McCracken, NSBA President; Molly Brogan Day, NSBA Vice President of Public Affairs; Kyle

Kempf, then NSBA's chief lobbyist; and to NSBA Board Members, Dick Herring, Larry Nannis, and Janet Kerley.

If I could, I'd like to hand out gold statuettes for distinguished service to the environment to this hearty band of small business leaders:

- Mark H. Clevey, former Executive Director, Small Business Foundation of Michigan; Vice President for Entrepreneurship of the Michigan Small Business Association;
- Scott Hauge, Founder and President of Small Business California;
- Jerry Lawson, Director of EPA's Energy Star Small Business program;
- Chris Lynch, Director of the Business Environmental Program at the University of Nevada;
- Chad Moutray, formerly the chief economist and director of economic research for the Office of Advocacy at the US Small Business Administration; now chief economist for the National Association of Manufacturers;
- Hank Ryan, former Executive Director of Small Business California and the organization's energy guru; and
- Thomas M. Sullivan, Vice President of Small Business Policy at the US Chamber of Commerce.

The alternate universe that is small business is boundless, ceaselessly dynamic, and teeming in its diversity. You can imagine how hard it is to reach this universe with some new message. The NSBA folks and all the individuals named above were unstintingly generous to me as I toiled to hoe this row. Bless their hearts, I say!

Lastly, I take pleasure in lavishing praise on Elaine Pofeldt, an independent journalist who specializes in writing about careers and entrepreneurship. Elaine is a former senior editor at *Fortune Small Business* magazine. Presently she's a *Forbes.com* contributing writer.

Elaine Pofeldt is the author of *The Million-Dollar, One-Person Business: Make Great Money. Work the Way You Like. Have the Life You Want* (Random House, January 2018). The book describes many entrepreneurs who are hitting seven-figure revenue in businesses *where they are the only employees*. Yes, they exist, and in abundance. Elaine has tracked them down and told their stories — not just of financial success, but of career satisfaction, and personal growth as well.

My personal and professional relationship with Elaine is long-standing and one of the joys of my career. She and I co-authored *SMALL WONDERS, How the Creative Drive of Entrepreneurial Small Businesses is Combating the Recession, Creating New Jobs and Economic Growth, Solving Energy Problems, Combating Global Warming, and Protecting the Environment*

Excuse my boasting, but I'm exceptionally proud of this 2009 report of the Center for Small Business and the Environment. I regard it as *the best thing on the subject that exists in print*. That's saying a lot I know, but perhaps not so much as you'd think. *There is nothing else like it in print.*

Here is a review of the report written by Greg Smith, for *Issuu*, a digital publishing platform. The review says it all, and every word rings true!

"Small Wonders is the first assessment that's ever been made of the widespread and proliferating phenomenon of small green businesses. The report describes a thriving new world of enterprise and innovation that's been largely hidden from view because small green businesses are so decentralized, diverse, and dynamic. But when viewed as a whole these firms are revealed as agents of profound change, revolutionizing technology, transforming culture, and realigning the political debate."

And, finally, to close here on an especially hopeful note, I'd like to acknowledge the anonymous young man I saw in a photograph of a student demonstration demanding action to combat climate change. The sign he held aloft read, "Don't worry adults! We'll take it from here!"

Appendix #1

Honor Roll: My Green Pioneers

Social movements are, of course, multifaceted. Looking back now, I can see that what I did back in the 1960s and 1970s was but one facet of an infinite number. But that doesn't make what I did *unimportant*. No way!

To the contrary, I'm now going to show you just how vital and pivotal my facet was. To do so, I've done something interesting and different. Countless acts? Countless actors? Bet your ass! But — guess what? — I've *counted* all the acts performed by my facet! And I've *counted* all the actors too!

Furthermore, I've described these actors, and in most cases, I cite a distinctive contribution made by each of them to the evolution and success of the environmental movement. Now, mind you, I'm *not* taking credit for all these wondrous deeds. But we were all part of a shared collaborative process — my facet!

As you review these names, bear in mind that this list is *entirely personal*. I make no claim to speak for the whole of environmentalism's history, just my little piece of it. But — I should emphasize — describing my little piece of the action serves to illustrate *how the whole operated*.

Please note that this list of green pioneers is restricted to the names of people I *personally* knew and worked with in the 1960s and 1970s. This was when the modern environmental movement was formed in the obscure nooks and crannies of society. This was when environmentalism acquired the massive force that allowed it to erupt and engulf the whole world and change it for the better.

George Alderson

Social movements are *political* movements; and, to succeed, social movements require able — even extraordinary — political leadership. But unlike professional politicians — virtually all of whom place their *personal* interests first — social movement politicians *must place the interests of the cause first.*

This sounds Pollyanna-ish, I know; but, believe me, such upright and unselfish souls exist and in abundance too. From its inception, the environmental movement benefitted from the integrity and dedication of such political leadership.

This brings me to George Alderson, whom I trot out here as Exhibit A.

When Friends of the Earth was formed in 1969, George came on board as the organization's legislative director. He was among the first environmental lobbyists to emerge in the nation's capital. Thank goodness, George and his counterparts were present and raring to go after Earth Day hit the big time in 1970. The event's huge political success landed in their laps like a gift from heaven, and they made the most of it, bless their hearts.

George also worked as a lobbyist for the Wilderness Society. In 1979, he wrote and published a handbook on being a citizen lobbyist, *How You Can Influence Congress.*

A forward-looking politician, George played a big part in getting environmentalists to form broad-based coalitions, involving labor unions, senior citizen groups, public health groups, minority groups, and inner-city residents.

Barbara Reid Alexander

In 1968, Barbara got her first political experience working on the Presidential campaign of Robert Kennedy. She and I were colleagues at the Conservation Foundation in the late 1960s where she was the assistant to Martha (Muffy) Henderson, a distinguished conservation educator.

Then in 1970, Barbara joined the fledgling Earth Day operation, becoming the Midwest Coordinator for the event. In the decades that followed, she became a leading consultant on consumer and environmental protection.

After ten years as Director of the Consumer Assistance Division at the Maine Public Utilities Commission, Barbara opened her own consulting practice in 1996 as a Consumer Affairs Consultant. She has represented public advocates and consumer organizations in over 30 states on public utility regulation.

As a result of her work, Barbara Alexander is one of a very few nationally recognized experts on consumer protection policies for residential consumers in public utility regulation.

Lawrence J. Amon

Like other enterprises, environmental organizations — to survive — need competent managers. Indeed, it may be that environmental organizations depend on competent managers *more* than other enterprises. That's because green groups are usually founded by high-minded enthusiasts, and high-minded enthusiasm doesn't always translate into prudent, sober organizational management.

Thank heaven, I say, for the Larry Amons of the world! Let's give them a shout-out!

Larry is a dedicated environmentalist, but he's also a dedicated financial manager. He's spent 45 years managing environmental organizations and managing them well.

His career has encompassed work at three major environmental organizations. As a senior staff member, he has guided the finances of The Conservation Foundation/World Wildlife Fund, the National Wildlife Federation, and the Ocean Conservancy.

Larry's love of nature got its start in the late 1950s when he was ten years old. That was when his family moved to the fairly undeveloped subtropical Sanibel Island, FL, where he had the run of the island and its beaches. It was heavenly.

Coincidentally, many years later, while he was at The Conservation Foundation, a staff member there wrote *The Sanibel Report*, a case study in how to develop a barrier island to optimize protection of its wildlife habitat. Sanibel now has a National Fish and Wildlife Refuge named after National Wildlife Federation's founder and first president, J.N. "Ding" Darling. This historical connection is a source of much pride and satisfaction to Larry.

Larry is retired now and living back on his beloved island where he has long maintained a home.

Gordon Binder

My old friend Gordon Binder certainly qualifies as a Green Pioneer — and then some.

Like many others listed here, Gordon was an Earth Day participant in 1970, helping organize a "teach-in" on the campus at the University of Michigan where he was an architectural student. And, like many others, he vowed to devote himself to ensuring the environment, the land, and other resources on which we depend remain productive.

Then it was just a hop, skip, and a jump to a summer internship at the new Council on Environmental Quality (CEQ) in Washington, DC, where he worked on a report on the inner-city environment, anticipating the later evolution of the environmental justice movement.

At CEQ, he met William Reilly, with whom he was to work closely for years, including assignments at The Conservation Foundation and World Wildlife Fund. When Reilly became Environmental Protection Agency (EPA) Administrator during the first Bush Administration, Gordon was appointed the agency's chief of staff.

Now, being chief of staff at the world's largest regulatory agency is undeniably a position of great power and authority. It's the sort of post that excites the awe and admiration of political denizens in the Nation's Capital — not to mention their envy.

But it's also a demanding job, 12-hour workdays and 7-day workweeks. The desk of the chief of staff is where the buck stops. No problems with easy solutions land there.

Here's what really interests me about Gordon Binder:

Gordon served as EPA chief of staff for four years — exercising "power" — and when he left the post, he *renounced* power. He'd had it. Instead, he chose to pursue his passion for art. And that's exactly what he's done.

Gordon has continued to play an advisory role in environmental policy. His judgement is highly regarded by dozens of environmental leaders. (I scarcely make a move without checking with him first.)

He is now a Senior Fellow at World Wildlife Fund, continuing to follow a range of issues, including land conservation. Recently, he's been involved with a project at American University on the future of environmental policy.

Gordon is a member of Studio Gallery in Washington, DC. His art displayed there features cityscapes and landscapes — (hey, that's *environmental*, isn't it?)

A final note: Gordon's reputation as an administrator lives on. A great many EPA old-timers still regard him as the best chief of staff the agency ever had.

Brent Blackwelder

Brent Blackwelder, then a student, was one of the countless people who turned out to participate in Earth Day in 1970 and who was inspired to commit his life to environmental protection. In 1973, Brent was founding chairman of the American Rivers Conservation Council. Later, this organization became American Rivers, which has a remarkable record of accomplishment.

Today American Rivers is working to:

- Protect 5,000 new miles of Wild and Scenic Rivers and one million acres of riverside lands;
- Remove 400 hazardous and outdated dams, restore 10,000 miles of rivers and 1,000 acres of floodplains;
- Reduce pollution in 100,000 miles of rivers and improve clean water for one-third of all Americans.

American Rivers now has 355,000 supporters.

In the early days, Brent joined Friends of the Earth, first as a volunteer; and, years later, he became its president, serving from 1994 until his retirement in October of 2009. (*Interns everywhere should take note of this. You too can rise to the top!*)

Lucy Blake

I like people who focus on some specific chunk of the Planet Earth, and who give all they've got to protect and preserve it. Lucy Blake has done that. She's rescued the Northern Sierra from destructive "development."

Lucy has been a passionate conservationist for almost forty years. Professionally, she began her career serving as Executive Director of the California League of Conservation Voters in the 1980s.

A native Californian, Lucy has been a prime mover in efforts to protect and preserve the magnificent natural landscape of the Northern Sierra. This is an area located in the northern portion of the Sierra Nevada mountain range. It stretches from Lake Tahoe to the southern border of the Lassen National Park.

She's now the President of the Northern Sierra Partnership which works with private landowners, public agencies, nonprofit organizations, and local communities, in a collaborative effort to restore and enhance the magnificent natural landscape and to build a foundation for sustainable rural prosperity.

The Partnership invests in land conservation, forest restoration, recreation, and sustainable tourism.

Prior to that, Lucy was Founder and President of the Sierra Business Council, an association of over 500 businesses working for the economic, social, and environmental health of the Sierra Nevada. The organization is based on the principle that business and environmental interests are more often coincident than in conflict, particularly in geographic areas where economic sustainability depends on environmental quality.

Lucy Blake was made a MacArthur Fellow in 2000.

Walter Bogan

I met Walter Bogan when he was Executive Director of the Scientists' Institute for Public Information (1965-1972) and working to bridge the gap between scientists and the media. Then he served as Director of the US Office of Environmental Education (1972-1982) where he endeavored to broaden the program so that students were exposed to the cultural, economic, and legal aspects of environmental problems and issues.

Ken Bossong

Who's Ken Bossong? Here's who Ralph Nader says he is:

"If Mother Sun were to select a *favorite son* on Planet Earth, Ken Bossong would be high on the list. Operating for over forty years on a tiny budget from a tiny office in Takoma Park, Maryland, the unsung solar energy advocate has been a one-man informing and organizing machine."

Ken founded the Sun Day campaign in 1992, in his words, "to aggressively promote sustainable energy technologies as cost-effective alternatives to nuclear power and fossil fuels."

With renewables like solar and wind energy becoming the fastest growing sources of new energy in many areas of the world, Bossong is now seeing his long and often frustrating battles against the traditional corporate skeptics increasingly vindicated.

Steadfast and serious, Ken Bossong calmly steeps himself in the startling statistics put out by the Federal Energy Regulatory Commission and the US Energy Information Administration, which are showing that nuclear power is rapidly losing the race with renewable energy sources.

Ken observes that, "Everyone loves a horse race. However, the smart money is now on renewables to soon leave nuclear power in the dust."

Joan Martin-Brown

Joan Martin-Brown claims that, during her career, her secret allies were Machiavelli and General George Patton, not bad choices for a feisty, independent woman trying to make her way in the 1960-70s patriarchal culture of Washington, DC. Her allies served her well. The woman got ahead in the world.

I met Joanie in 1977 when Doug Costle, just chosen by President Carter to be EPA Administrator, hired her to head the agency's Public Affairs Office. She did a bang-up job! During her time at EPA, Joanie:

- Vastly expanded the agency's outreach to the public, including labor, the agriculture community, state governments, business and industry, NGOs, women, religious leaders, and youth;

- Produced EPA's first Citizen Participation Guidelines;

- Launched the *EPA Journal*, a highly respected government publication and one that actually made money;

- Commissioned a GAO audit of major hazardous waste sites in rural and urban areas and their adjacent demographics. The findings documented that powerless, minority populations were the most exposed, and this information helped inform the environmental justice movement;

- Joined with the Department of Energy to underwrite the cost of the first Harris Poll on US attitudes on energy conservation and the environment.

Joanie later spent twelve years representing the United Nations Environment Program to the US. There she initiated the "World Industry Conference on Environmental Management" held in Versailles. She also organized regional UN assemblies on women and the environment in Egypt, Zimbabwe, Thailand, and Ecuador. And, in her spare time, she founded World Women in Defense of the Environment (WorldWIDE), a not-for–profit organization.

During the last eight years of her career, Joanie continued to launch breakthroughs, this time at the World Bank. As Senior Advisor to the bank's Vice-President, she initiated the Greening of the World Bank project, a giant step in getting the bank to incorporate environmental concerns into its operations, something it had long resisted. Not a bad way to wrap up a career.

Joanie wishes to thank Machiavelli and General Patton for helping her climb the ladder of success. She also sends her affectionate regards to Mother Teresa.

Lester Brown

What's a *guru*? A guru is a teacher, sure; but often the word means *more* than a teacher. In Sanskrit, the classical language of India, *guru* means the one who dispels the darkness and leads us towards the light.

Now, in my day, I've heard numerous environmental leaders called gurus, but I won't name names for fear of embarrassing people. However, I'll make an exception for Lester Brown. He's been called "the guru of the environmental movement" by no less than *The Telegraph of Calcutta,* a large daily newspaper in India, so they should know what they're talking about.

In any case, speaking for myself alone, I'm more than willing to call Lester a guru. He's dispelled a lot of darkness for me; and, if I have seen any light, he's certainly one of the people who got me to see it.

In 1974, Lester founded the Worldwatch Institute, the first research institute devoted to the analysis of global environmental issues. Worldwatch soon came to be regarded as one of the best sustainable development research organizations in the world.

I was awed by the work that Worldwatch did. They had a terrific staff, everyone of them smart as a fox. My friend, Bruce Stokes, a brilliant writer and researcher, worked there.

In particular, I treasured their publications, *The Worldwatch Papers*, which provided cutting-edge analysis on complex environmental issues and which trotted out — and relied on — the best available science. I counted these papers as a source of my (much needed) continuing education about global environmental issues.

Thank you, Les! Thank you for your guru-ship!

Lester Brown has authored or coauthored 54 books. His books have appeared in 40 languages. His most recent book is *The Great Transition: Shifting from Fossil Fuels to Solar and Wind Energy*. In 2013, he published his autobiography, *Breaking New Ground: A Personal History*.

Lester Brown retired in 2015, at the age of 81.

Lynne Cherry

Lynne Cherry is the author and illustrator of over thirty books that teach children respect for the earth. Her best-selling books, such as *The Great Kapok Tree* and *A River Ran Wild*, have sold over a million copies and have been translated into many languages.

Her most recent book is *How We Know What We Know About Our Changing Climate: Scientists and Kids Explore Global Warming*.

William A. Drayton

One of the pleasures of taking part in a social movement is that you get to work with a lot of *very smart* people, even some — I daresay — who qualify as *brilliant.* Select company, indeed!

My select company includes a fellow named Bill Drayton who is one of the smartest guys I ever met and, moreover, one of the ablest.

(I've been jealous of him practically from the day we met.)

Bill is perhaps best known for coining the phrase "social entrepreneur" — a now-famous phrase used by cognoscenti the world over.

(Why the hell didn't I think of this?!)

The concept of social entrepreneurship reflects Bill's faith in the power of a person with a good idea to tackle not just a social problem but also *the systemic forces that cause such problems.* As Bill defines it, "Social entrepreneurs are not content just to give a man a fish or to teach him how to fish. They will not rest until they have revolutionized the fishing industry."

(This bon mot of his has been quoted zillions of times — some might say to the point of ad nauseam.)

Bill has the street cred it takes to pull off such a high-wire act because he himself is a social entrepreneur with a long record of tackling and solving problems.

(Common decency compels me to state this, otherwise I'd skip it!)

I met him in the 1970s when he was serving in the Carter Administration as an Assistant Administrator at the Environmental Protection Agency.

(Even then he was going around wowing people with his brains and talent. What a show-off!)

At EPA, he introduced the concept of emissions trading, a fundamental change in how we attempt to reduce pollution. Sometimes referred to as "cap and trade," it has been used successfully to cut harmful sulfur dioxide emissions from power plants that decimated Adirondack park lakes for years and offered new options to reduce water pollution. Emissions trading also has inspired programs and proposals to cut climate warming CO2 emissions.

(Okay, okay, so he's had a good idea once or twice!)

In 1980, Drayton founded Ashoka: Innovators for the Public, a public interest organization dedicated to finding and fostering social entrepreneurs worldwide. In the years since, he's served as Ashoka's CEO, overseeing the evolution of social entrepreneurship into a global force for good — an association of over 3,900 Ashoka Fellows. More than 1,000 of these Fellows focus on the environment.

By funding the work of social entrepreneurs around the world, Bill Drayton has addressed and alleviated problems ranging from human rights abuses to climate change to poverty.

(Can you believe the nerve of this guy?! Where does he get off?)

Someday, if I live long enough, I hope to catch up with him.

Louise Dunlap

From 1976 until 1986, Louise was President of the Environmental Policy Institute and Environmental Policy Center, groups she co-founded in 1972 and which, under her leadership, became highly respected environmental lobbying organizations in Washington.

Louise created and led the seven-year national citizens' effort to enact the Surface Mine Control & Reclamation Act of 1977, which requires the coal industry to protect valuable farmlands, streams and wetlands, and to reclaim all surface mined lands. Louise continues to be a principal strategist and advocate for community groups working to reclaim abandoned mines and to obtain enforcement of surface mining laws.

Marion Edey

Among environmentalists, Marion Edey is a living legend. She was present at the movement's creation and pivotal in the movement's acquisition of formidable political clout. In 1970, Marion founded the League of Conservation Voters (LCV). That makes her a Green Pioneer about ten times over.

It's not too much to say that LCV was her brainchild. In 1969, Marion, then a young Congressional staffer, proposed creation of a non-partisan national pressure group for environmentalists "analogous to a political party" but endorsing Democrats *and* Republicans. David Brower and other environmental leaders seized on the idea, and it took off.

Marion served as LCV's national coordinator from 1970 to 1986.

The organization's main activities include voter education, voter mobilization, tracking voting records, endorsing or opposing candidates for political office, and financially contributing to political campaigns.

Since 1994, LCV has helped elect and re-elect 73 US senators and 330 members of the US House of Representatives. The organization now has more than 2 million members across the country – an increase of nearly 150% since 2012.

In the mid-term election in 2018, the LCV Victory Fund invested $85 million to help elect pro-environment leaders — the largest investment by any single-issue group. And what a big pay-off they got!

Sixty new members of Congress were elected, and the US House went from being *anti*-environmental to *pro*-environmental. At state and local levels, the result was just as mind-blowing. Eleven states elected new green governors. Nearly 300 new pro-environment state legislators were elected across the US.

So, when I think of LCV *victory signs* start flashing inside my head. That's a brainstorm I welcome. Thank you, Marion Edey!

My favorite memory of Marion is not political, however, but theatrical. In an early edition of the Public Interest Follies — the satirical revues we left-wingers produced during the Reagan years — she wrote and performed a skit that tickles me still when I think of it.

In the skit, Marion, who was then a director of Friends of the Earth (FOE), declared that she had decided to withdraw from the organization because its political stance was much too radical. She'd just formed, she announced, a new organization that would advocate more moderate positions than FOE. This organization, she proudly declared, would be called *Acquaintances* of the Earth.

Brock Evans

Brock Evans, a legendary figure in the environmental movement, is someone I greatly admire. He played a major role in the campaign to save Washington's North Cascades in the early '60s, thus beginning his environmental career. He's been a leader in achieving protection of Hells Canyon, the Boundary Waters Wilderness, and many other natural areas around the country.

He was the Northwest representative of the Sierra Club from 1967 to 1973, until he moved to Washington, DC to head the Club's lobbying office, a position he held until 1981. Brock then worked for 15 years with the National Audubon Society, where he served as lobbying director and vice president for national issues.

Brock is the author of *Fight and Win,* a prize-winning book about how environmentalists can succeed politically. He is now President of the Endangered Species Coalition. He is currently working on his autobiography, *Endless Pressure, Endlessly Applied.*

Sharon Francis

In these pages, I've bent over backwards time and again to proclaim the historical consequentiality of the environmental revolution. *Everything was changed for the better!* But there's a pivotal chapter in this story I haven't yet told. I'm going to tell it now (and with some relish, since — as luck would have it — your humble author is part of the story).

This is the stupendous story of Ladybird Johnson's "beautification" program — an initiative which critics back then derided as trivial — planting flowers and picking up trash — but which — almost *subversively* — forged a basis for the soon-to-come global revolution in environmental consciousness. In the panoply of environmental heroes, I place Ladybird Johnson right up there alongside Rachel Carson.

Thank Heaven, telling this story, we have an eyewitness account to draw on. Indeed, we have the best person left alive on earth to tell the story: Sharon Francis, Mrs. Johnson's assistant for beautification.

Sharon, a native of Seattle, was an avid mountain climber for most of her life. In 1959, she graduated in political science from Mount Holyoke College where she wrote her honors thesis on the wilderness bill. In 1961, her writings in national conservation publications caught the attention of Stewart Udall, the new Kennedy administration's incoming Secretary of the Interior. Udall asked Sharon to become his ghostwriter.

In 1964, when the First Lady, Ladybird Johnson, told Udall about her intention to launch a beautification project, he sent Sharon to the White House to help out. She joined the East Wing staff in March of 1965 and remained there through the end of the Johnson Administration in January of 1969.

Here's where I come in. (You needn't applaud.) I was then working for the Interior Department's Bureau of Outdoor Recreation — specifically on the staff that had been assigned to develop and support Ladybird Johnson's beautification program.

In this position, I worked closely with Sharon who, like me, was enamored by the (then newly minted) ecological worldview. We were like religious disciples then, passionate advocates, determined to spread the new gospel far and wide.

We had an ally. Ladybird Johnson was one of us.

Operating under the rubric of "beautification," Mrs. Johnson defined her project broadly — *very* broadly. She started by focusing on "highway beautification": planting wildflowers along the sides of roads, reducing the number of billboards, and masking the sight of automobile junkyards and landfills.

But beautification was soon to embrace the preservation of national parks and the protection of the countryside. Then it expanded to include the improvement of inner-city neighborhoods, the restoration of playgrounds, and the preservation of historic sites and areas.

Please note the significance of Ladybird's wide embrace. Under the rubric of "beautification," the world of conservation — parks, recreation, wildlife, wilderness preservation, etc. — was linked to the urban environment. *This was for the first time!* Back then the world was divided up. Earth Day in 1970 was to bring it back together. Mrs. Johnson was a herald of things to come.

Ladybird knew what she was doing. She was deeply worried about pollution, urban decay, the need for outdoor recreation, setting the stage for good mental health, improving public transportation, and on and on. She said so, eloquently:

"Though the word beautification makes the concept sound merely cosmetic, it involves much more: clean water, clean air, clean roadsides, safe waste disposal and preservation of valued old landmarks as well as great parks and wilderness areas. To me ... beautification means our total concern for the physical and human quality we pass on to our children and the future."

Sharon and I worked together on the White House Conference on Natural Beauty in 1965, which President Johnson convened to promote Ladybird's project. Henry Diamond was Executive Director of the Conference. He was a close personal friend of Sharon's and of mine. And he was a green pioneer par excellence and a founder of the environmental law movement. (See my tribute to him later in this appendix.)

I am so proud to have been part of that time and that endeavor. Sharon Francis remains a heroine to me still.

After she left the White House, Sharon moved to New Hampshire where she coordinated the New Hampshire-Ohio acid rain partnership in the 1980s and founded and directed the NH Natural Resources Forum from 1983 to 1997.

In 1990, she became executive director of the newly formed Connecticut River Joint Commissions, legislatively designed to foster cooperation between Vermont and New Hampshire on issues related to the conservation and management of a shared natural resource.

In 2004, Sharon received the Teddy Roosevelt Conservation Award from President George H. W. Bush.

Sharon is now writing her memoir, *Trail to the White House and Trails Beyond.* I've been privileged to see some draft chapters from this memoir, and I must tell you that, reading them, I was overcome with nostalgia. Her intimate and frank account of those years recalled to me a time when people in power cared terribly about the things I care terribly about. May such a time come again!

Joseph Breckinridge Handy IV

Joe Handy possesses a Green Pioneer credential that's hard to match.

Newly graduated from college, he began his career at the newly formed US Environmental Protection Agency *on its first day of operation, December 2, 1970.* How's that for getting in on the ground floor?

His time at EPA lasted through the Administrations of Nixon, Ford, Carter, and almost two and a half years of Ronald Reagan.

I met him in 1977 when my pal, Joan Martin Brown, was hired by Doug Costle to run EPA's public information office. Joe was her principal assistant. Before I met Joe, I remember an excited Joanie telling me about her new assistant. "Byron," she said, "this guy can do anything!"

I've known and worked closely with Joe in all the years since, and I'm happy to report that Joanie was right. *Joe Handy can do anything!* (For instance, he designed and produced this book.)

In the agency's early days, EPA was a very exciting place to work. Countless smart, ambitious, and highly motivated young people flocked there to launch careers in environmental protection. Joe was in the right place at the right time. He had some great assignments.

Joe oversaw the design and staffing of the new Visitors Center which was to take up the entire first floor surrounding the entrance to the newly opened EPA headquarters in DC. In 1974, he represented EPA at the World's Fair in Spokane, the first environmentally themed world's fair. Two years later, he was in charge of designing and staffing the EPA Pavilion at that year's World's Fair, the Bicentennial Expo on Science and Technology at the Kennedy Space Center in Cape Canaveral, FL. He later toured the United States with a portable EPA traveling exhibit featuring photos from the now widely hailed, DOCUMERICA program.

Having been born and raised near the ocean in Long Beach, CA, his dream to live near the beach was realized by relocation to Venice Beach in the 1990s. Joe married his life-long friend Mark Crosby, and they continue their commune with nature, a block from the beach with a small California garden, a fish pond, and a talking parrot named Diego.

Peter Harnik

Peter Harnik was for many years National Coordinator of Environmental Action, the organization established immediately after Earth Day in 1970 to handle the follow-up to the project's massive success. It seemed as if the whole world wanted to get into the act — which daunted Peter not in the least. "Bring it on," was his mantra.

Peter is the founder of the Center for City Park Excellence at the Trust for Public Land (TPL), which he directed until his retirement in 2016. He authored *Inside City Parks*, a book about the park and recreation systems in the 25 largest US cities.

Previous to TPL, he was co-founder of the Rails-to-Trails Conservancy along with David Burwell. Their leadership inspired a movement that has led to more than 20,000 miles of rail-trail around the country. These pathways run the gamut of uses and styles—from dirt trails through pristine wilderness to paved pathways through our biggest cities—and are enjoyed by tens of millions of Americans every year. Peter is currently writing a history of the rails-to-trails movement in the United States.

For my part, however, I like mostly to think of my pal, Peter Harnik, as "Mister Bike." A tireless cyclist, he served as president of the Washington Area Bicyclist Association for many years — in which capacity he raised a lot of hell in defense of biking and bikers. Many motorists in DC hate his guts.

I can't be absolutely sure of this, but I estimate that — over the years — the number of miles ridden by Peter on his bike is the equivalent of encircling the globe three times. (I'll work on the figures and get back to you.)

And finally, this: Peter is the only person I know who has a park bench named after him. It's on the Capital Crescent Trail in the District of Columbia, and it's the only park bench to found there, a lonely distinction, but well deserved. I hope all the hikers and bikers who rest their tired asses there will take a moment to say, "Thanks, Peter!"

Denis Hayes

Denis and I go back a long way.

I first met him in 1969 after he was named National Coordinator of the Environmental Teach-In, Inc., by its sponsor, Senator Gaylord Nelson. (The "teach-in" had not yet evolved into Earth Day.)

Decades later, speaking at the 40th anniversary reunion of Environmental Action, Denis told a story that still warms my heart. He said that when he first took on the job, he feared the event would turn out to be just another wave of demonstrations by radical students on college campuses.

That's not what he had in mind.

Then Denis described how relieved and pleased he was when I walked in and told him about the network of civic coalitions I had formed around the country, working as a community organizer for the Conservation Foundation. These coalitions were filled with people from groups like the League of Women Voters, the United Auto Workers, state and local affiliates of the American Lung Associations, high school science teachers, and Boy Scouts and Girl Scouts.

This was *exactly* what Denis had in mind.

Denis and I hit it off, and we worked together for years.

Some years later, Denis had the idea for Sun Day, a national celebration of solar energy, modeled on Earth Day. He got President Carter to designate May 3, 1978, as a day to be specifically devoted to advocacy of solar power. And he got Congress to pass a joint resolution authorizing Sun Day as well.

Denis served as National Chair of Sun Day. He invited me to serve as National Vice-Chair, which I gladly agreed to do. Sun Day took off! Countless events were held throughout the country and in thirty other nations.

Then, in 1979, Denis asked me to take on the job of organizing a national commemoration of Earth Day's tenth anniversary. (At the time Denis was Director of the Federal Solar Energy Research Laboratory, a federal employee, so he couldn't take on the job). That's how I became National Chair of Earth Day '80.

Denis is the author of several books. The most recent (and perhaps most popular) is *Cowed: The Hidden Impact of 93 Million Cows on America's Health, Economy, Politics, Culture, and Environment* (2015), written with his wife, Gail Boyer Hayes.

Denis has been acclaimed repeatedly for his many services to the environment. But, perhaps, since he's a small-town boy, the most satisfying is this:

In 2007, the town of Camas, Washington, where Denis grew up, renamed the high school in his honor. In 2015, the street outside of the Denis Hayes High School was renamed Denis Hayes Street.

Hazel Henderson

In 1960, as a young housewife in Manhattan, Hazel Henderson noticed that when she left her windows open her curtains were dirtied. When she complained to the city health department about this, she was told not to worry, "it was just mist blowing in from the sea."

Hazel didn't buy this, not for a second. Instead, she went out and co-founded Citizens for Clean Air in New York City, one of the first anti-pollution groups in America and, for her, the start of a long and wide-ranging political and intellectual journey.

Today, Hazel Henderson is a world-renowned futurist, a science policy advisor to many governments, and a television producer with eight published books to her credit, and a globally syndicated newspaper column.

She is the founder of Ethical Markets Media, LLC, which promotes the emergence of a sustainable, green, more ethical, and just economy worldwide.

This fabulous career originated back in the 1960s when Hazel realized that to make her case for clean air stick, she'd have to tackle and unravel *economics,* a daunting task for a young woman who'd not attended college. No matter, Hazel determined to learn economic theory *on her own.* This she did — and, as a result, economics will never be the same. And Hazel went on to receive four honorary doctorates!

Here's why: Hazel's central idea is that traditional economic theory is not really a neutral science but is actually politically motivated. To me, her propagation of this idea is her grandest achievement.

The environmentally concerned housewife has managed to *unmask economics* — a profession which presents itself to the world as a scientific discipline. In fact, there is nothing at all scientific about economics since it lacks testable hypotheses. In economics, there is no such thing as a controlled experiment, given the boundless, uncontrollable complexity of economic phenomenon.

Hazel argues that many economists use the trappings of science — dense mathematics, for example — to trick people into thinking they are engaged in pure science (And, perhaps, I should think, to justify the big bucks they charge for providing "scientific expertise.")

Hazel alleges that economics is a disguised form of politics, one that always comes out favoring the interests of the rich and powerful. She calls economics "a form of brain damage." For this achievement, I think she deserves to win the Nobel Prize in Economics.

What a great joke this would be, for as Hazel delights in pointing out, *there is no Nobel Prize in Economics!* Alfred Nobel (1833-1896) did not create one. He established prizes for chemistry, physics, and medicine, which *are* sciences.

The economics prize was established in 1968 by a donation to the Nobel Foundation from Sweden's central bank, Sveriges Riksbank. Its official name is The Sveriges Riksbank Prize in Economic Sciences in Memory of Alfred Nobel. Note the reference to "Economic Sciences."

So, the con game continues. Alfred Nobel must be spinning in his grave.

John Heritage

Earth Day is almost unthinkable without John Heritage and the key role he played in making it happen. His involvement was no accident of fate. John was where he wanted to be and deserved to be.

In 1967, working as a reporter for the *Minneapolis Star Tribune*, John created the newspaper's environmental beat. Then a series he wrote about environmental degradation in Minnesota was nominated for a Pulitzer Prize.

Then in 1970, he was working as the environmental assistant for Minnesota's Senator Gaylord Nelson. So, when Nelson got the idea for a national environmental "teach-in," he asked John to spearhead the effort.

As I recall, he was the glue that held everything together, one of several unsung heroes of the environmental movement.

Later in his career, John edited *The EPA Journal*, the magazine of the Environmental Protection Agency, from 1979 to 1993.

John Hunting

What a remarkable fellow John Hunting is! First, he puts his money where his mouth is, and then he gives his money away! And we ain't talking chickenfeed. We're talking $100+ million.

John was the founder and President of the Beldon Fund, a foundation committed to building the political power of the environmental movement, particularly at the state level. The $100+ million came from first the profits, and then the sale of, Hunting's stake in Steelcase Corporation, a leading office furniture manufacturer co-founded by John's father.

After the $100 million gift, John declared that Beldon would spend out all its assets over ten years. The foundation focused on making grants to highly innovative projects — taking risks and not playing it safe.

Beldon closed its doors at the end of May 2009 and is an example — a rare example — of philanthropy practiced the way it should be. To me, it's a worthy model that other philanthropists might adopt, and thanks to John's tireless efforts since Beldon's closing, many have.

Wes Jackson

"The plowshare may well have destroyed more options for future generations than the sword," declares Wes Jackson, a revered leader in the international movement for a more sustainable agriculture.

"Wes Jackson," an admirer has said of him, "has taken it upon himself to speak for the grasses and the land of the prairie, to speak for the soil itself."

Wes, who was born and raised on a farm near Topeka, KS, is co-founder of The Land Institute in Salina, KS. The institute was launched on 28 acres in 1976 by Wes, a plant geneticist, and his wife Dana, a food activist.

The Land Institute seeks to integrate food production with nature in a way that sustains both. Specifically, the institute develops alternatives to current destructive agricultural practice which are dependent on heavy chemical applications and petroleum consumption, and which leads to soil erosion and degradation.

- The institute is dedicated to advancing *perennial grain crops*, a concept modeled after the ecological design of prairies that are known for their soil quality, deep root systems, and self-sufficiency.
- The institute also promotes *polyculture farming solutions*, which reduce soil erosion and inputs of irrigation, fossil fuels, fertilizers, and pesticides.

Under Wes's guidance, Land Institute scientists are cross breeding the annual crop plants — wheat, sorghum, sunflower, and legume — with wild, perennial relatives to create perennial varieties. Using selective breeding and other techniques, they also are working to domesticate wild perennials

Wes Jackson is the author of *New Roots for Agriculture* (1980); *Becoming Native to This Place* (1996); *Consulting the Genius of the Place: An Ecological Approach to a New Agriculture* (2010); and most recently *Nature as Measure: The Selected Essays of Wes Jackson (2011)*.

"If we don't get sustainability in agriculture first," Wes declares, "sustainability will not happen."

Wes Jackson retired in 2016.

Mike Jacobson

In 1971, Michael F. Jacobson founded The Center for Science in the Public Interest (CSPI) along with James Sullivan and Albert Fritsch — all of whom had worked at Ralph Nader's Center for the Study of Responsive Law. Today, CSPI is perhaps the oldest independent, science-based consumer advocacy organization in the nation. For almost a half-century, the organization has provided practical advice to consumers interested in nutrition, food safety, and health. This has paid off big-time.

The work of Mike Jacobson and CSPI has succeeded in changing the way Americans think about food and even the way they eat. Mike successfully led efforts to ban trans fat and reduce sodium levels in the food supply.

We have him and CSPI to thank for the Nutrition Facts labels that now appear on packaged foods, showing what nutrients are in the food. CSPI's work has transformed the food quality in schools, restaurants, grocery stores, and public places.

This is a good place to mention that CSPI co-founder Jim Sullivan and I collaborated extensively back in those days. Together, we started the National Council for the Public Assessment of Technology in an effort to ensure that ordinary citizens were given a say in the process of technology assessment.

Merle Lefkoff

I met Merle Lefkoff in the late 1960s when I was helping organize the environmental movement in the state of Georgia. She was then just an ordinary housewife raising four children, getting a PhD at Emory University in Atlanta, and, in her spare time, working her tail off to protect her home state's magnificent natural environment.

Joining forces with then-Governor Jimmy Carter, Merle helped steer sand dunes protection legislation through the Georgia Legislature, the first such legislation in the nation. She was also Executive Director of SUNREP, a non-profit advocacy organization for solar and alternative energy use in the Southeastern US. In the early 1970s, she founded and was President of Save America's Vital Environment (S.A.V.E.), a lobby set up to promote the then-emerging environmental movement.

"The Pearl," as her intimate friends call her (I am one), is one hell of a change agent. She's unstoppable. Merle will improve society whether society wishes to improve or not. And she has energy to burn.

The word "dynamic" doesn't begin to define her style. On top of that, Merle is one of the most delightful people to work with I've ever encountered. She makes saving the world fun. I adore her.

In 1976, when Jimmy Carter was elected President, (she was a prominent volunteer in his campaign) she hightailed it to Washington, DC. After serving for a year in the Carter White House on a special detail, Lefkoff set up a full-time consulting practice in 1978. Her many clients since have included the Congressional Office of Technology Assessment, the Environmental Protection Agency, the Army Corps of Engineers, the Department of Energy, Interior's Bureau of Land Management, and Agriculture's Forest Service.

Basically, what Merle's done in the course of her career is a remarkable and singular public service. She's trained generations of government administrators in the art and science of environmental conflict management.

Typically, these folks are highly competent technocratic bureaucrats who badly need what Merle has to offer. She teaches them how to hear, understand, respect, and learn from their critics outside government, especially concerned citizens and environmental advocates. In the end, everybody comes out ahead. What a grand achievement!

Over the years, Merle has traveled the world, employing her special talents in assisting conflict resolution in many venues for various groups. She has been a mediator, facilitator, and leadership trainer in conflict zones around the world. In the last few years, Merle's attention has been fixed on a growing world-wide network of civil society groups, scientists, and young activists, alarmed over the implications of climate change and species extinction, perhaps the most important among the many challenges we face. As a social change entrepreneur, she founded and is Executive Director of the Center for Emergent Diplomacy, which is dedicated to meeting the challenges of the climate catastrophe that is now upon us.

Catherine Lerza

Back in the old days, Cathy Lerza was a one-woman social change whirlwind. She edited *Environmental Action* magazine and the book, *Food for People, Not for Profit.* She co-founded and directed the National Family Farm Coalition and also served as associate director of the Rural Coalition.

As a grant-maker, she was executive director of the San Francisco-based Shalan Foundation and the Washington DC-based Beldon Fund. Cathy was a senior philanthropic advisor at Tides Foundation, helping lead its environmental, civic participation, and reproductive justice programs.

Cathy is also a professional actor, working regularly in film and video and on stage in the Bay Area. I've seen her perform and, take my word for it, she is *absolutely fabulous!*

Sam Love

Sam Love, a community organizer, was the Southern coordinator for Earth Day in 1970. After Earth Day he became editor of *Environmental Action* magazine.

Sam is a splendid writer who has published two novels and three books of eco-poetry. His newest book, *Awakening: Musings on Planetary Survival,* has been published by England's Fly on the Wall Press. The book has been nominated for the prestigious Laurel Prize, which honors books of eco- and nature poems.

Accordingly, my tribute to him here is written in the best doggerel I can manage.

Sam, the fellow who organized Earth Day
In the verdant American South,
Talks in a way that's a verbal bouquet;

He could summon the birds
With the beauty of words
Which flow, like a song, from his mouth.

Now, when right-wingers balk
At ecology talk, and squawk
When he's hawking enviros;
Sam fashions a dart to toss at their heart:
In order to show 'em, he writes a fine poem,
And conquers their heart with his art.

Amory Lovins

I wonder what it's like to be Amory Lovins. I wonder what it's like to be — early on — *very, very right about something very, very important*?

What's it like, I wonder, to bring critical new knowledge into a world that *resists* absorbing critical new knowledge? A world that would rather bury its head in the sand than learn something new?

Glory be! — what's it like to succeed at such a Herculean task? To teach the world something that is new and vital, in an existential sort of way?

My old friend, Amory Lovins, has done all this.

Amory is not a guy who goes around bragging about his many admirable accomplishments. He doesn't need to: they speak for themselves. Surely, in his secret heart of hearts he must be bursting with pride. Who wouldn't be? I'd be off the charts! Maybe even insufferable!

(Note to Amory: the next time you're in town let me know, and I'll buy you a drink and quiz you on all this. I promise not to fawn.)

A tour de force! Amory launched his career in 1971 as the British representative for Friends of the Earth. (That's when I met him.) In the course of his career, he's managed to focus the world's attention on alternative approaches to energy and transportation. (I'd call that achievement *Herculean*, wouldn't you?)

Amory's critical thinking, his analysis, his communication skills have driven people around the globe — from world leaders to the average Joe and Jane — to think differently about energy, not to mention its role in climate change, oil dependency, national security, geo-politics, economic well-being, depletion or pollution of the natural resources on which we depend.

In 1982, Lovins and then wife Hunter founded the Rocky Mountain Institute (RMI). RMI investigates ways to increase the efficiency and sustainability of resource use, working with governments, industry, and society to help achieve this. Over the years, RMI has churned out solution after solution.

Amory has always focused on approaches that conserve natural resources while also promoting economic growth. His thinking is colossal, profound, pioneering. He aims to get us off oil and coal by 2050 — saving, in the process, $5 trillion! This can be accomplished, he argues, without an act of Congress, but through businesses seeking profits.

"Public discourse about climate change has resulted in the erroneous idea that it's all about cost, burden, and sacrifice," Amory declared. "If the math was correct, everyone would see it's about profit, jobs, and competitive advantage."

Amory Lovins, a Harvard and Oxford dropout, is the author of 31 books and more than 600 papers. He's received eleven honorary doctorates.

He is a modest man.

L. Hunter Lovins

If a vacancy opens up for the position of Wonder Woman, I'd like to nominate Hunter Lovins for the post. She could do the job with one hand tied behind her.

Hunter Lovins has been called a "Hero for the Planet" (*Time*) and "a green business icon" (*Newsweek*). She's won the Right Livelihood Award, the Rachel Carson Award, and the European Sustainability Pioneer award.

Hunter began her green pioneering in the early 1970s, when she was a law student. She helped establish the urban forestry and environmental education group, California Conservation Project (TreePeople), and was its assistant director for six years. TreePeople inspires and supports people to come together to plant and care for trees. Over the years, the organization has planted millions of trees in the Los Angeles area.

In 1982, Hunter and her then-husband Amory Lovins co-founded the Rocky Mountain Institute (RMI) in Colorado. The institute was established to accelerate the adoption of market-based energy solutions that make the shift from fossil fuels to efficiency and renewables.

Amory and Hunter initially ran the institute out of their home and referred to it as a "think-and-do-tank." In the 1980s, RMI grew into an organization with a staff of around fifty. Hunter served as the institute's Chief Executive Officer for Strategy until 2002. (Today RMI has approximately 229 full-time staff, annual operations of $56 million, and a global reach and reputation.)

Hunter is the President and Founder of Natural Capitalism Solutions (NCS), a non-profit she formed in 2002. NCS helps companies, communities, and countries implement more regenerative practices profitably. It is one of the most influential environmental policy analysts in the world.

Hunter, a professor of sustainable business management at Bard College, teaches green entrepreneurship and coaches green social enterprises around the world.

She operates in the belief that citizens, communities, and companies, working together within the market context, are the most dynamic problem-solving force on the planet. Her message is pragmatic and positive.

"If we use resources productively and take to heart the lessons learned from coping with the energy crisis, we face a future confronted only, as Pogo once said, by insurmountable opportunities. The many crises facing us should be seen, then, not as threats but as chances to remake the future so it serves all beings."

Hunter has written 16 books, including the recently released *A Finer Future: Creating an Economy in Service to Life* (2018), a winner of the Silver Nautilus Award.

Francesca Lyman

Francesca Lyman is everything you could hope for in an environmental journalist. She's serious, thoughtful, reliable, thorough, objective, and an exemplar of professional integrity and decorum.

Plus, she can sing and dance like nobody's business — and in *public* too. I can attest to this personally. I have sung and danced with Francesca on stage numerous times, and — what's more — in front of live, large, and *appreciative* audiences. And — not to brag — but the reader should know these audiences paid *good money* for the privilege of seeing us perform. No kidding!

I met Francesca when we were performers in The Public Interest Follies, a community theatre group Peter Harnik and I organized to produce satirical revues during the Reagan years.

The large (and loud) left-wing community in DC loved our shows. They flocked to see us. And we had fans too! They even made local "stars" out of Francesca and me.

(I'll get in deep doo-doo here if I don't mention the names of other Follies "stars": Ligeia Fontaine, Karen Friedman, Peter Harnik, Cathy Lerza, Mike McCabe, Susan Robson, and Bruce Tobin. And I'm bound to get in deep doo-doo with others whose names I've failed to mention.)

In the Follies, we performed rib-tickling skits about such topics as endangered species, deforestation, ocean pollution, and, of course, the then-emerging controversy of global warming. A skit about the ozone hole in the late 1980s — called *The Perfect Tan* — featured sun-bathers traveling to an imaginary Club Med located in Antarctica for the fastest-acting bronzing job on the globe.

Whoa! What am I doing? I've wandered completely off the subject! Forgive me!

I should get serious! After all, this piece is supposed to be about Francesca Lyman's sterling career as an influential and prominent journalist. I should point out that she's the author of *The Greenhouse Trap: What We're Doing To The Atmosphere And How We Can Slow Global Warming,* with the World Resources Institute (Beacon Press, 1990). That's one of the very first books ever written on global warming!

Francesca's career began as a newspaper reporter in New Jersey in 1979 when she covered the transportation of radioactive waste on local roads in the wake of the Three Mile Island nuclear meltdown. She also covered local news and personalities, paying attention to topics like hazardous waste buried under school yards as a staff writer for the *Passaic Herald-News* of New Jersey.

During her career, Francesca has covered everything from acid rain and toxins in baby bottles to the carbon footprint of Valentine's Day flowers.

Her resume is extensive: She was an editor of Environmental Action magazine from 1980 to 1986. She wrote the award-winning Your Environment column for msnbc.com for 7 years. Plus, she's published two books, including a children's book about the Central African rainforest, and has been a contributing writer for publications like *The New York Times*, *Los Angeles Times*, *The Washington Post*, and many magazines and websites.

In 2012, Francesca was the recipient of a Fund for Environmental Journalism grant from the Society for Environmental Journalism, while working as a columnist for *The Sacramento Bee* and, in 2016, an Arlene award for journalism "making a difference" from the American Society of Journalists and Authors.

Although she has long since hung up her dancing shoes, Francesca continues to practice environmental journalism. She's now working as an investigative reporter for *InvestigateWest*, a nonprofit journalism organization in Seattle.

W. Michael McCabe

From 1975 to 1976, Mike McCabe served as legislative assistant to Senator Gary Hart, specializing in environmental and energy policy, including the promotion of energy efficiency and renewable energy. From 1976 to 1979, he also served as Staff Director of the bipartisan Congressional Environmental and Energy Study Conference.

In 1980, at the behest of Denis Hayes, Mike and I joined forces to organize Earth Day '80, the national commemoration of the tenth anniversary of Earth Day, me as National Chair and Mike as Executive Director. We both worked our butts off on this project, which occurred at a time when much of the national press had turned on the environmental movement, a total reversal from 1970 when the press was eating out of our hand. And in April 1980, unbeknownst to us, the nation was about to be engulfed by the Reagan revolution. But Mike and I emerged from this trying experience with a bond of friendship that will last forever.

Mike went on to achieve a distinguished career. From 1981 to 1985, he served as Staff Director of the US House of Representatives Energy Conservation and Power Subcommittee. In 1995, McCabe was appointed by President Clinton as the Regional Administrator of the EPA Middle Atlantic Region. In 1999, President Clinton nominated him as EPA Deputy Administrator and Mike was appointed to that position in 2000.

McCabe is currently the Principal at McCabe & Associates, in Chadds Ford, Pennsylvania, a private consulting firm addressing energy and environmental policies.

Former Congressman Paul N. ("Pete") McCloskey

A highly decorated Marine during the Korean War, McCloskey was one of the nation's first environmental lawyers. He represented California's 11th District in Congress from 1967 to 1983. In 1970, McCloskey became the cochairman of the first Earth Day. In 1973, McCloskey co-sponsored the Endangered Species Act. Pete continues to practice law and protect the environment. He lives on an olive and walnut farm in Northern California with his wife Helen Hooper McCloskey.

Richard Munson

Dick Munson's green pioneering career was launched in the 1970s when he worked as the coordinator of the Environmental Action

Foundation. That's when I first met him. In 1978, he was co-coordinator of Sun Day, an international celebration of alternative energy modeled on Earth Day. In the past, he also served as Executive Director of the Solar Lobby and Executive Director of the Center for Renewable Resources.

As a clean energy advocate, Dick packs a one/two punch. He scores his points politically, and he scores them historically. It so happens he's damned good at doing both. Between the two, he gets his point across.

As an advocate of clean energy, for example, he served as senior vice president at Recycled Energy Development, a Chicago-based enterprise that seeks to cut greenhouse-gas emissions by advancing efficiency and capturing and recycling waste energy.

As a historian, he's the author of *The Power Makers,* a history of the electric power industry. One reviewer described this book as "the most entertaining and informative guide to one of America's most important industries. It shows that business as usual doesn't work, and that a new generation of electricity entrepreneurs can supply the technological innovation this country needs."

The Power Makers was also hailed as "a sober and thoughtful analysis of the troubled electricity business" by *Washington Monthly* and ranked by them as one of the best political books of the year.

Dick is also the author of *From Edison to Enron,* another take on the history of the energy industry. Here again, I can't do better than quote a reviewer:

"An extraordinarily comprehensive and enjoyable historical portrait of the nation's most critical energy supply system, and its indispensable engine of progress and prosperity. This splendid book is as readable as it is rigorous in its fascinating journey through the creation and the evolution of the electricity enterprise in the 20th century. What set Munson's work apart is his probing exploration of the powerful and diverse personalities who collectively shaped what has become the world's largest and most complex machine." (2005)

Dick's latest book, *Tesla: Inventor of the Modern*, was published by W.W. Norton in October 2019. Again, I cite a review:

"Tesla invented the radio, robots, and remote control. His electric induction motors run our appliances and factories. Tesla worked tirelessly to offer electric power to the world and to introduce automatons that would reduce life's drudgery, yet he has been largely overlooked by history. In Tesla, Richard Munson presents a comprehensive portrait of this farsighted and under-appreciated mastermind."

Dick is now Director of Regulatory & Legislative Affairs for the Environmental Defense Fund based in Chicago where he advocates for clean energy in the Midwest. He works to protect competitive electricity markets, modernize the grid, and advance the clean electrification of vehicles and buildings.

J. Henry Neale, Jr.

Environmentalism is a social movement whose greatest strength lies in its pervasive decentralization. This is how we confound — and beat the pants off — the fossil fuel boys who've pretty much got a stranglehold on the operations of the centralized state.

In the American constitutional system, no governmental entity is conceived to be more pivotal than the states. Basically, that's where the Constitution begins. And, at this level, the environmental movement has labored to make itself felt — and with considerable success. I think there is one or more environmental advocacy organizations in the capitol of every state of the union. Where would we be without them?

I treasure these state efforts, and I salute them, each and every one. In many ways, they are the heart and soul of the movement.

Here — to honor them all — I've chosen to tell the story of the leader of one such notable statewide effort. Henry Neale exemplifies everything I'm talking about.

Henry is a green pioneer who has spent the last half-century fighting to protect the natural environment of his beloved home state, New York. In 1969, Henry, a lawyer in Scarsdale, was among the founders of the organization that was to become the Environmental Advocates of New York, the primary environmental government watchdog in Albany.

In the decades since, Henry has retained an affiliation with the organization, serving in many capacities, from President to various committee chairs. Today, he's a member of Environmental Advocates Advisory Board and a director of their action fund.

Environmental Advocates monitors state government, evaluates proposed laws, and champions policies and practices to benefit the environment, conservation, wildlife, and public health in New York State. The organization has been an effective one. No good law it supported has ever been repealed; no bad bill it opposed has been adopted; and, it always fights tenaciously during the annual State budget process to obtain adequate funding for worthy programs, such as Environment Protection Fund.

Environmental Advocates helped secure passage of some of New York's key environmental laws, including:

- the state's bottle deposit law
- the nation's first acid rain law
- wetlands protection
- Hudson River Estuary Management Act
- Lead Poisoning Prevention Act

• Clean Indoor Air Act

Environmental Advocates is now battling to combat climate change while encouraging the development of clean green energy technologies. It's leveraging new financial support for conservation efforts. And it's laboring to clean up badly polluted land sites in order to get those properties back on tax rolls.

Perhaps the highlight of Henry's environmental advocacy is this: for nine years, he led an alliance which fought to obtain adoption of the Returnable Beverage Container Act ("the Bottle Bill"). And they won! This was a rare legislative victory by citizen advocates going up against vigorous opposition by well-funded industry lobbyists.

Henry was elected to the Clearwater Board of Directors in 2017. Clearwater was founded by Pete Seeger, legendary musician, singer, songwriter, folklorist, activist, environmentalist, and peace advocate. In 1966, in despair over the pollution of his beloved Hudson River, Seeger announced plans to "build a boat to save the river."

The sloop Clearwater — a majestic 106-foot long replica vessel – was launched in 1969. It is recognized as America's Environmental Flagship and is among the first vessels in the US to conduct science-based environmental education aboard a sailing ship, creating the template for environmental education programs around the world.

Today, Henry's primary interest is at the local level. He's spent years of service with the Federated Conservationists of Westchester County. He's served as Chair of the County Environmental Management Council. Recently, he was appointed Chair of the County Parks, Recreation and Conservation Board.

Henry and his late wife, Sue Higgins, also an indomitable environmentalist, enjoyed much time in their beloved country home in Columbia County, where they were strong supporters of the Columbia Land Conservancy.

Jacquelyn A. Ottman

I hereby award the prize for the earliest launching of a green career to Jacquie Ottman. At age four she dragged home abandoned board games from the neighbor's trash and insisted that her parents salvage them.

When Jacquie went to high school in the early 1970s, she was declared the school's "Recycling Czar." And, like many people profiled in these pages, she participated in Earth Day in April 1970 where she was so moved that — on the spot — she committed her life to the cause of the environment.

It should come as no surprise that Jacquelyn Ottman pioneered green marketing.

Jacquie started her career learning the marketing ropes while working for Procter & Gamble and Ralston Purina. Then, in 1989, sparked by awareness for the role of consumer goods in environmental issues, she founded J. Ottman Consulting, Inc. Her goal was to bring the same disciplined approach used by savvy marketing pros to the development and marketing of environmentally preferable products and services.

Since then, Jacquie has helped over 60 of the Fortune 500 find competitive advantage by leveraging credible green marketing and eco-innovation strategies. Clients include 3M, GE, Johnson & Johnson, Epson, Nike, and Samsung.

Jacquie's first book was *Green Marketing: Challenges & Opportunities for the New Marketing Age* (1993) which was hailed as "definitive text on the subject" by the American Marketing Association. Since the she has published *Green Marketing: Opportunity for Innovation* (1998) and *The New Rules of Green Marketing* (2010).

When it comes to green marketing, Jacquie is not only the first word on the subject, *she is the last word too.*

In 2018, she published *If Trash Could Talk*, the world's first collection of verse about the stuff we throw away. Jacquie says the book is intended to amuse anyone who's ever taken home a doggie bag, rummaged through a vintage sale, or unabashedly served a leftover.

She's now going to cooking school and writing a book on the three "R's of Leftovers" - reduce, reheat, and repurpose. Her wish is to start a new tradition in America, "Leftover Pooling Night" — a clean out the fridge night, if you will.

Here's how she writes it up in *If Trash Could Talk.*

Leftover Pooling

What's old to me is new to you.
At least that's what I'm banking on in a new tradition
I'm starting, called "Leftover Pooling,
The new Sunday night feast in every home in America."
Just like it sounds,
Find some friends, family, and neighbors,
And pool what's left in everyone's fridge.
Fill in with a salad or dessert,
And have fun sharing more than just leftovers.
Start with recounting the week's adventures
Through the meals you prepared,
Enjoyed in a restaurant,
Ordered from a new take-out place.
New dishes you discovered in a new ethic place,
A recipe you dug out of the drawer.
And savor the magic that transpires from there.

Today, Jacquie is focused on changing consumption culture in her native New York City as founder of the website WeHateToWaste.com and as a member of the Manhattan Solid Waste Advisory Board.

Chris Palmer

Chris Palmer is an environmental/wildlife film producer who has swum with dolphins and whales, come face-to-face with sharks and Kodiak bears, camped with wolf packs, waded hip-deep through the Everglade swamps, and jumped out of helicopters.

(Now, I'm too much of a wimp to attempt any of these things, but somehow, I still have the gall to call myself an environmentalist. Well, at least, I write *courageous* things. You should see some of my manifestos calling for radical action. Hair-raising stuff.)

Chris arrived in this country from Great Britain in 1972. He became active in the environmental movement and landed a job on Capitol Hill, working for US Senator Charles H. Percy, a liberal Republican who was a strong environmentalist. (Yes, such people existed back then).

When Jimmy Carter was elected President, Chris was a political appointee at EPA, serving as Chief of Staff to the Administrator and Deputy Administrator. That's when he and I met.

Chris's career as a film producer began in 1983. In the years since, he's spearheaded the production of more than 300 hours of original programming for primetime television and the IMAX film industry. His films have been broadcast on numerous channels, including Animal Planet, the Disney Channel, PBS, and TBS. His IMAX films include Whales, Wolves, Dolphins, Bears, Coral Reef Adventure, and Grand Canyon Adventure. He has worked with the likes of Robert Redford, Paul Newman, Jane Fonda, and Ted Turner.

Chris is now retired but has become a prolific author. Rowman & Littlefield recently published his seventh book, *Design Your Life for Success*. Occasionally, he performs stand-up comedy in DC area comedy clubs.

Rafe Pomerance

I first met Rafe back in the early 1970s when he was running the National Clean Air Coalition, a job that was plenty demanding. But he was soon to take on a job that demanded *heroism* -- and a hero he became.

If he wished, Rafe Pomerance could offer himself up as a living rebuke to America's dysfunctional and corrupt political system. How so? Because *decades ago* — starting in the late 1970s — he tried desperately to call attention to the risk of catastrophic climate change and humanity's role in causing it.

Oh, if only Rafe had been *heard*! If only he had been *heeded*! We wouldn't be in the rotten mess we are now, facing God-knows-what calamities. It should never have come to this! And it wouldn't have if advocates of climate action had been given a fair hearing, instead of being scorned and derided.

Now, Rafe wasn't the first person to sound this alarm. Scientists began taking detailed measurements of carbon dioxide levels in the late 1950s. Even back then, some scientists began warning that the accumulation of greenhouse gases might create problematic warming of the planet. Nobody paid them the slightest bit of attention.

Thus, it was that few people had heard of global warming when Rafe took up the issue in the 1970s. Rafe determined to change that, to get the word out *pronto*. The strategy he employed was a shrewd one. He trotted the scientists out, connecting them with government policymakers and with the media, and he kept at it. The story began to build.

But the fossil fuel industry soon struck back, launching an insidious disinformation campaign that scientists and environmentalists are still struggling to combat. Amazingly, the fossil fuel boys managed to peddle the false gospel of climate denial to masses of people, including many in the Republican Party.

Through it all, Rafe persevered. He was President of Friends of the Earth from 1980 to 1984, and then joined the World Resources Institute as a senior associate for climate change and ozone depletion policy. He went on to serve as deputy assistant secretary of state for environment and development in the Clinton administration and has since worked with numerous environmental and research organizations, including Woods Hole Research Center.

Today, at 72, Rafe is still going at it. He is now Chairman of Arctic 21, a network of organizations focused on communicating issues of Arctic climate change to policymakers and the general public.

Recently, a reporter asked him if his early efforts to combat climate change had been worth it. Rafe replied: "Oh, absolutely. Every bit of effort was worth it. I knew very early that this would become a dominating issue on the planet. We started out and nobody knew anything about it and now everyone does. Was it worth it? Absolutely!"

Carl Pope

I met Carl in the late 1960s when he was Political Director of Zero Population Growth. He went on to become one of the most important figures in the environmental movement.

Carl worked for the Sierra Club for more than 30 years, serving as Executive Director and then as Chairman, stepping down in November 2011. He is now the principal advisor at Inside Straight Strategies, focusing on the links between sustainability and economic development. He serves as a senior climate advisor to Michael

Bloomberg, with whom he authored *Climate of Hope, How Citizens, Businesses and Citizens Can Save the Planet* (2017), a New York Times bestseller.

The *Kirkus Review* sums the book up well. "In a time when national leadership seems bent on denying the facts of climate change and failing to plan for the likely consequences of it, the authors propose that smaller-scale efforts are more likely to produce the desired results, efforts that empower cities, regions, businesses, and citizens to accelerate the progress they are already making on their own."

Michael Rawson

Michael's love and appreciation of nature begin as a Boy Scout and — like so many of the other old-time greenies honored here — led to his participation in Earth Day when he was a college student.

After graduating from college in 1970, Michael lucked out, landing environmental jobs for the next 13 years. He worked first at the Council on Environmental Quality as a research assistant (1971-1972), and then at The Conservation Foundation, working in government affairs (1973-1982).

In 1982, Michael left the Conservation Foundation and his work directly on environmental policy but left behind neither his love of nature nor his commitment to preserving our natural world.

He became a day care teacher, taking care of the youngest among us while more and more parents have little choice but to work. He had a 25-year career in childcare (commonly known as day care) earning a graduate degree in early childhood education.

Caring for infants, toddlers, preschoolers, and five-year-olds, he would take them outside, introducing his young charges to the wonders of nature and the outdoors. In these mostly twice-a-day walks with the children, he discovered that children's interest in and love of nature is a universal, no matter the age or sex.

Michael understands that children today are going to inherit an earth vastly different and, in many ways, less hospitable than the one we have enjoyed. In his view, we are all entrusted with the responsibility of helping children learn how they can respond creatively, responsibly, and positively to this challenge.

Now retired, Michael is also an accomplished artist, having gotten his certificate of botanical art and illustration from the US Botanic Garden and the Corcoran Gallery School of Art. The beauty of nature is the focus of his art, and he's utterly entranced by trees.

William K. Reilly

Bill Reilly has been one of the most thoughtful environmental leaders of our time.

A former Republican EPA Administrator, I'm deeply grateful to him for struggling to keep environmental bipartisanship alive-and-well through thick and (mostly) thin. I'm grateful as well to the other former Republican EPA Administrators who've been part of this struggle: the late William D. Ruckelshaus, the late Russell E. Train, Lee M. Thomas, and Christine Todd Whitman.

As EPA Administrator under Bush 41, Reilly led the charge for a new Clean Air Act, which introduced a highly successful trading regime to reduce SO2. He triggered the veto of the Two Forks Dam in Cheeseman Canyon outside Denver, which remains a premiere fishing and recreation spot. He created the office of what was then called environmental equity and challenged the Agency to look more at place-based programs to address pollution problems. And he led the US delegation to the UN Conference on Environment and Development in Rio in 1992, where the climate convention was signed.

Reilly also served as a senior staff member at the newly created White House Council on Environmental Quality, as president of World Wildlife Fund and later chairman of the board, and as president of The Conservation Foundation.

President Clinton appointed Bill as a founding Trustee of the Presidio Trust of San Francisco. President Obama appointed him co-chair of the National Commission on the BP Deepwater Horizon Oil Spill and the Future of Offshore Drilling and, in late 2012, to the President's Global Development Council for which he headed the working group on climate smart food security.

Throughout his career, Reilly has retained a sense of humor and civility, grounded in a pragmatic view of what government and policy can achieve when well applied. Bill's an optimist at heart, which gives me reason to hope we can actually deal with climate change and other environmental challenges.

Ann Satterthwaite

Jane Jacobs hated city planners. The famed author of *The Death and Life of Great American Cities* (1961) defended the vibrancy and diversity of city life against the zeal of planners and Mayors intent on tearing down slums to build gigantic urban renewal projects.

Planners then thought that cities should be clean, orderly, and hospitable to automobiles and suburbanites. Jacobs, however, disagreed. In fact, she believed the very qualities that many city planners wanted to squash were what made cities desirable: quirkiness, variety, density, and self-regulating community.

The environmental revolution launched on Earth Day in 1970 supported and advanced Jane Jacobs's ideas. (It's worthwhile noting that she was a participant in the first Earth Day. She spoke at an Earth Week teach-in in Milwaukee where she made her case for decentralizing planning.)

Of all the professions upended and altered by the environmental revolution — and for *the better* — none was more so than *city planning*. The profession of *city* planning was transformed into the profession of *environmental* planning. A light year's difference!

This vast change is well exemplified by the long and prestigious career of my old friend Ann Satterthwaite. I met Ann when I went to work for the Conservation Foundation in 1968. At that time, she'd already been green pioneering for almost a decade.

In 1960, when she got her master's degree in city planning from Yale University, Ann decided to specialize in environmental planning. Basically, she wanted the planning process expanded to include more *conservation* benefits, more *recreation* benefits, and more *cultural* benefits.

That same year she went to work for the Outdoor Recreation Resources Review Commission, the Federal government's first national recreation study. Here Ann persisted in asking a simple question: how did the government's open space programs affect urban development? Yes, back then this simple question needed asking. Government programs needed to be taught how to put 2 and 2 together.

Later in the 1960s, Ann joined the Conservation Foundation, where she helped design projects aiming at showing how ecological principles could be blended into urban development, which — though it seems perfectly obvious now — was then almost a novel idea.

In the 1970s, Ann continued work on projects that defined and refined the profession of environmental planning. For example, she wrote the environment section of Colorado's State Plan. She wrote a report on the role of culture in outdoor recreation for the National Endowment for the Arts.

Through the years, Ann has steadfastly advocated for the protection of cultural landscapes. These are "combined works of nature and man" according to the World Heritage Committee — landscapes that have been especially influenced by human activity, such as Stonehenge, historic battlefields, and sacred Indian mounds. And through the years, she has sought to recognize and honor the heritage of Frederick Law Olmsted (1822-1903), the father of American landscape architecture.

Also, in the 1970s, Ann worked for the Appalachian Trail Conservancy on a project to protect the mountainside of the trail from Maine to Georgia — a project labelled the Appalachian Greenway. Now over 40 years later, this project has come back with a bang, and Ann is working on it again.

Throughout her career, Ann has labored to make historic and cultural preservation a major goal of environmental planning, and she's done so with considerable success, especially in Charleston, SC, where she prepared a report on future goals and programs for the Historic Charleston Foundation.

Perhaps the culmination of Ann's devotion to historic preservation is achieved in her most recent book, *Local Glories: Opera Houses on Main Street, Where Art and Community Meet* (2016). In *Local Glories*, Ann explores the creative, social, and communal roles of the thousands of opera houses that once flourished in small towns across the country. Sarah Bernhardt, Mark Twain, and John Philip Sousa entertained thousands of local townspeople, as did countless actors, theater and opera companies, innumerable minor league magicians, circuses, and lecturers, and even 500 troupes that performed nothing but *Uncle Tom's Cabin.*

Today, many communities across the country are restoring these opera houses and reviving their use — a splendid example of historic preservation that Ann joyfully celebrates.

Scott Seydel, Sr.

Scott Seydel, Sr. is Chairman & Chief Innovation Officer of the Seydel Companies, a leading manufacturer of innovative, specialty chemicals for over 100 years. The Seydel Companies were named EPA's Waste Wise Small Business Partner of the Year in 1999, 2000, 2001, 2002, 2006. This should come as no surprise.

Over the past four decades, Scott Seydel has devoted much of his career toward creating environmental awareness. He has chaired the Global Green board and serves as a Board Director of Mikhail Gorbachev's Green Cross (Geneva). He is chair emeritus of Elemental Impact and the GreenBlue Institute and a founder of its Sustainable Packaging Coalition. He is a former Board Member of the National Recycling Coalition and Vice Chair of the Container Recycling Institute.

Through his work with these organizations, Scott helped create The Coalition for Resource Recovery.

Scott Sklar

If I'm going into a fight over renewable energy, I'm going into it with Scott Sklar at my side, or I ain't going. He's the champ! What Babe Ruth is to baseball, what Joe Louis is to boxing, what Charlie Chaplin is to screen comedians, Scott Sklar is to renewable energy.

Scott was in renewable energy *before it was invented*. When he got started, people just referred to "the sun" or "the wind." Now, thanks largely to Scott, people all over the world talk about *solar energy* and *wind power*.

(Of course, I'm just joking, but only *just*.)

Scott gave me a tour of his house once, pointing out the many renewable energy devices he's added, from micro wind turbines on the roof to solar shingles to a fuel cell inside. After a serious hurricane one year disrupted power in his neighborhood, he was the only one who had power, thanks to those devices.

He told me the local fire department asked to store items in his refrigerator and he was happy to do it. What a great demonstration of micro power!

It's no wonder the fossil fuel boys hate Scott's guts. They can't win a debate with him! He's got all the facts on his side, plus he's inexhaustible. And he puts on a good show too. The man is a born entertainer. When he's debating energy issues, a lot of people stick around just for the jokes. (*Did you hear the one about the traveling solar panel salesman?*)

Sklar began his energy career years ago working as an aide to New York Senator Jacob K. Javits. During his Senate tenure, he co-founded the Congressional Solar Caucus which led to much innovative legislation promoting renewable energy in the 1970's.

In the years that followed, Scott served as Political Director of the Solar Lobby and Executive Director of the Solar Energy Industries Association.

Scott Sklar is now President of The Stella Group, Ltd. a business that promotes and facilitates use of distributed energy systems that are clean and super-efficient. He also now serves as Adjunct Professor at The George Washington University.

James Gustave Speth

In the early days of the environmental movement Gus Speth seemed to be everywhere at once. What a mover and shaker he was! And, now, a half-century later, he's still at it.

And while he moves fast, he leaves monuments behind him, impressive ones.

In 1970, he co-founded Natural Resources Defense Council. In the late 1970s, under President Carter, he chaired the US Council on Environmental Quality. Then in 1982, he founded and became president of the World Resources Institute.

From 1993 to 1999, Gus was Administrator of the United Nations Development Program. From 1999 to 2009, he served as Dean of the Yale School of Forestry and Environmental Studies. He is now a Professor of Law at the Vermont Law School.

Gus has written several books, including *The Bridge at the Edge of the World: Capitalism, the Environment, and Crossing from Crisis to Sustainability* which *The Washington Post* regarded as "one of the best books of 2008" ... in the Nature & The Environment category.

His latest book, a memoir, *Angels by the River* (2014) traces his path from mainstream environmental insider to a champion of fundamental systemic change in our political and economic institutions. So, Gus is *still* shaking things up.

A statement he made recently went viral and has been quoted zillions of times. It is worth quoting here.

"I used to think that top environmental problems were biodiversity loss, ecosystem collapse and climate change. I thought that thirty years of good science could address these problems. I was wrong. The top environmental problems are selfishness, greed and apathy, and to deal with these we need a cultural and spiritual transformation. And we scientists don't know how to do that."

The reason I quote this here is because I was profoundly moved by Gus's sentiments and the honest expression of his despair. His statement is one of the reasons I wrote this book. It reflects my personal search for a cultural and spiritual transformation. I found much to comfort me; I hope it comforts Gus.

Lola Van Wagenen

Lola Van Wagenen, a consumer activist and environmentalist, was co-founder of Consumer Action Now (1971) in San Francisco, which helps underrepresented consumers assert their rights in the marketplace. The organization just celebrated its 48th anniversary.

In 1972, Lola organized the Environmental Action Forum, a gathering place for consumer and environmental activists. From 1975 to 1977, she developed The Sun Fund as a tool for raising awareness of energy conservation and alternative energy sources.

I met her when she served on the Task Force on Appropriate Technology with the US Office of Technology Assessment in 1977.

In 1978, we worked together on Sun Day, a national celebration of solar energy, modeled on Earth Day. I was National Co-Chair of the event, and Lola was Sun Day's organizer in New York City, where she did a bang-up job. The celebration began with a sunrise ceremony at the United Nations.

For three days, people in New York City could scarcely escape hearing about the glories of solar energy. Television blanketed various Sun Day events. Lola lined up noteworthy people to speak, like Margaret Mead, Dr. Barry Commoner, Pete Seeger, Amory Lovins, and her then-husband, actor Robert Redford.

Lola's mantra was: "Earth Day identified the problems; Sun Day identified the solutions."

In 1979, she received an Honorary Doctorate in Science from the Pratt Institute for her promotion of energy conservation and renewable energy.

Michaela L. Walsh

The mighty environmental revolution turned the world topsy-turvy, changing everything. Old assumptions fell by the wayside. New assumptions popped up everywhere. The environmental revolution made connections possible that weren't possible before — or even *conceivable.*

Here's where Michaela Walsh waltzed in. Her great contribution back in the 1970s was to connect women + entrepreneurship + environment. Who'd ever thought these could fit — and work — together? As I recall, Michaela was first to see the connection. But then making unusual connections was her forte. It still is.

Now, if we talk today about the role of women entrepreneurs in environmental protection, the subject isn't likely to raise any eyebrows. The idea doesn't sound so strange. That's because Michaela and her colleagues have succeeded in selling the concept to the world. Good for them!

However, speaking as an old-timer, I can tell you that — in the early days before everyone's environmental consciousness had been raised — hearing Michaela's formulation was like a flash of lightning, revealing an astonishing new landscape of possibilities, causing us to *ooh* and *aah* in surprise and admiration.

So, Michaela's vision was very exciting. It built a bridge between two powerful and growing movements for social change: feminism and environmentalism. What's more, this formulation — *if realized* — would lead to economic opportunity and new jobs for women.

So, Michaela went out and did it! Here's how.

In the late 1950s, Michaela was one of the few women working on Wall Street.

In the 1970s, she became the first woman to make partner at the Wall Street brokerage firm Boettcher and Company. She later joined the Rockefeller Brothers Fund, working on projects to improve the economic status of women. This led her to attend the United Nations World Conference on Women held in Mexico City in 1975. Here the idea of Women's World Banking (WWB) was born.

WWB was founded to help women entrepreneurs around the world gain access to credit, so they could own their own businesses. To achieve this, WWB built a global network of women-owned financial institutions committed to serving local women. WWB has fostered a culture — from Kenya to Colombia to the Philippines— wherein women entrepreneurs can learn from and teach each other and gain control over their economic destinies.

Michaela was a co-founder of Women's World Banking and its first president, a position she held from 1980 to 1990.

WWB has focussed on assisting women who are working to achieve a more sustainable, environmentally friendly life for people in their communities. One example is support of women in India who are developing an infrastructure of distributed renewable solar energy in rural areas of their country.

Michaela's book, *Founding a Movement: Women's World Banking 1975-1990*, published in 2012, is invaluable social history. It describes how, in the days before WWB, the presence of women in the economy was invisible — statistically and officially. And it describes how WWB boldly asserted and established women's economic rights in the realm of formal banking.

Geoffrey Webb

Geoff Webb won his first green credentials doing hard labor. In 1977, he spent six months rehabilitating back-country trails when working for the Young Adult Conservation Corps of the US Forest Service. He says he's not been in such good shape since.

Later, Geoff worked as an intern in the House of Representatives where he was assigned to the office of Congressman Paul N. ("Pete") McCloskey, a Republican who had been national co-chair of Earth Day in 1970. Then he worked as a renewable energy advocate for the Solar Lobby.

During his long career, Geoff has worked for public interest organizations, philanthropic foundations, State governments, and the Federal government, including a stint as Deputy Director of Congressional & Intergovernmental Affairs at the Interior Department.

Geoff's always been a great political strategist and a shrewd, pragmatic operator. He got things done. I've been impressed with him ever since I first met him. He was then the chief lobbyist and political director of Friends of the Earth in Washington, DC. Geoff was elected to FOE International Executive Committee and served from 1985 to 1989.

However, Geoff is perhaps best known as a Friend of the *West*. That's his native region, and that's where his heart is set. Over the years, he's been a behind-the-scenes mover-and-shaker of more Western conservation initiatives than you can shake a stick at.

This record includes the establishment of more than two dozen national monuments, wilderness areas, and designated wild and scenic rivers. He played a key role in the designation of the Grand Staircase-Escalante region in southern Utah as a national monument. The region is among the most remote and beautiful landscapes in the country.

Geoff has served as a state official in New Mexico. He was the first Commissioner of New Mexico's Youth Conservation Corps and then served as Assistant State Land Commissioner. In this capacity, he represented the Land Office in the development of a NM State Energy Plan and a NM State Mining Law.

Geoff now heads up FoundationWest, a non-profit organization based in Santa Fe, NM, that is focused on issues of environment, justice, and democracy.

Kathleen Welch

Kathleen Welch has three decades of advocacy, campaign, and philanthropic experience behind her. For nearly a decade, Kathleen served in senior roles at the Pew Charitable Trusts, overseeing investments in climate and clean energy advocacy and serving as deputy director of the Environment Group.

Kathleen currently serves on the advisory council of the Brainerd Foundation in Seattle, which provides conservation-related grants in the Pacific Northwest. She also serves on the boards of the League of Conservation Voters and the Natural Resources Defense Council.

Kathleen is now a principal at Corridor Partners, a firm headquartered in Washington, DC, and New York, where she is focused primarily on advising donors regarding advocacy and political strategies on climate and clean energy issues.

Carol & Jack Werner

I love people who get in on the ground floor of a new social movement. I love even more people who *create* the ground floor of a new social movement. There's just one catch: movement-creators must be prepared to work terribly hard for no pay and, usually, for a long time.

In these early stages, there are *no* paid jobs to be had, *no* foundation grants to apply for, and *no* government contracts to seek. And, since typically society does not welcome new movements for social change with open arms, the prospects for fame are as slim as those for fortune.

Now, I know that — to a lot of people — laboring in obscurity at hard work for no pay sounds like a prison sentence. And yet — hallelujah! — the world is full of people who do just that! These dear souls give their all, in service to a noble cause without much hope of getting anything in return for themselves personally. In the early days, the environmental movement was loaded with such people — and still is!

Allow me to introduce Carol and Jack Werner.

Carol Pencook (from Iowa) came to DC in 1970 to start grad school at GWU. She started working on the Hill in 1971. Jack Werner (from Nevada) came to DC for an internship in the Senate in 1972. As a kindly fate would have it, these two budding greenies met, married (in 1974), and determined — between the two of them — to make the world a better place. In this, they have succeeded.

Carol and Jack have spent their careers in the energy, environment, and climate nexus through a variety of non-profit organizations, as well as their stints working on Capitol Hill.

Carol led the Environmental and Energy Study Institute's energy, climate, and sustainability work for 32 years. Jack has worked for years with state and local governments, including serving as the director of Washington DC's energy office, to showcase innovation and best practices in energy, environment, and transportation.

Jack's passions were shaped by his three years (1967-1970) in the Peace Corps in Gabon and Liberia. There he worked with local communities to build the roads, bridges, wells, schools, etc. they sorely needed. There he learned about — and used— *appropriate technology.*

What is appropriate technology? The term describes technologies that are small-scale, decentralized, labor-intensive, energy-efficient, environmentally sound, and locally autonomous. Perhaps most importantly, the aim of appropriate technology is to make needed and beneficent technologies available and affordable to the world's poor.

Jack Werner found his higher calling in appropriate technology, and he responded to the call with his whole heart and soul. He had a great — and wildly ambitious — idea for promoting the concept. He would organize a gigantic exhibition of appropriate technologies — a fair, no less — and he would do it on the National Mall in Washington, DC. He went to work, and he pulled it off! The only catch: he had to slave around the clock for a year without earning a dime.

(During this long stretch, the Werners lived off Carol's then munificent annual salary of $15,000. She was then the legislative director of the National Abortion Rights Action League.)

So much for the sacrifice! Let's focus on the *triumph!*

ACT '79: Appropriate Community Technology Conference & Fair was held on the Mall on April 27-30, 1979. A virtual community was built to showcase a broad array of appropriate technologies. As they say, it takes a village. ACT '79's village included a town hall, grocery store, holistic health/wellness center, post office, etc.

There were exhibits on sustainable agriculture, including aquaculture, and a display of on-site composting techniques for small gardens. There were also exhibits on urban gardens, food co-ops, and chemical free growing systems.

Most of the energy used on-site was *produced* on-site through use of small wind turbines, solar collectors, and bio-digesters.

More than 100,000 people participated in ACT '79. It was then the largest community-based technology fair ever and probably remains so to this day. The event got press coverage all over the world. I think ACT '79 put appropriate technology on the map.

A joint Senate/House Congressional hearing was held, chaired by Rep. Richard Ottinger (D-NY), at which First Lady Rosalyn Carter testified. This hearing inspired Majority Leader Jim Wright to launch a similar fair in Dallas/Fort Worth the following year. Several other regional ACT events were held across the country over the next few years.

(The Werners wish to credit Tina Hobson and the late Bill Holmberg, who were then both high-ranking officials at the Department of Energy and who provided financial assistance and leadership support to Jack's efforts.)

I see the legacy of ACT '79 as immense. Thanks to the fair, at least in part, environmentalists the world over share what I'd call *a philosophy of technology.*

This philosophy calls for a technology that is small in scale, not large; a technology that emanates from the bottom up, not from the top down; a technology that is controlled locally, not nationally.

This philosophy of technology blends environmental stewardship with social and economic justice. The great promise of appropriate technology lies in its practical effects. This promise, if realized, means that, for example, poor people in the Third World will no longer have to cut down trees in order to have wood to burn as fuel so they can boil water to make it safe for drinking.

CITATIONS
FOR DISTINGUISHED SERVICE
TO THE ENVIRONMENT

In the winter and spring of 1970, dozens more green pioneers turned up on the scene as April 22 approached. The Washington, DC office, where I helped out, was an exhilarating madhouse — crowds rushing in and out; all the phones ringing off the hook.

Then, on the day after Earth Day, it seemed like the floodgates of humanity had been opened. It seemed like half the world wanted to be environmentalists!

Instantly, Environmental Action was organized to handle this flood of aroused humanity. To recapture this moment in environmental history, I've done the best job I can of recollecting the names of the people who were then part of the scene. (My apologies to those whose names I've inadvertently left out.)

Here I laud them all — named and unnamed — for their service to the cause.

Earth Day 1970 Staff & Key Volunteers (Washington, DC office)

Barbara Reid Alexander	Dick Dalsemer
Eric Amrine	Andrew Garling
George Coling	Steve Haft
Kent Conrad	Bryce Hamilton
Stephen Cotton	Michael Harris

Denis Hayes
Vic Key
Robert Lilley
Sam Love
Bill Mark
Robin Moyer
Carol Parker

Tom Plumb
Arturo Sandoval
Jan Schaeffer
Doug Scott
Frank Wallick
Ruth Wallick
Lucky Wentworth

Environmental Action

Environmental Action (EA) was one of the most vibrant organized efforts ever undertaken to green the planet. EA was launched on April 21, 1970 — the day *before* Earth Day — by the event's organizers. Overnight, the group went from organizing Earth Day to lobbying on Capitol Hill for giant steps in environmental protection. They scored giant gains.

EA combined political activism and grassroots organizing with an experimental egalitarian staff structure. Because of this, it was considered among the most radical of the national environmental groups.

EA originated the *Dirty Dozen* campaign. This campaign targeted members of Congress who were the most consistent opponents of environmental protection measures and who were judged to be the most vulnerable to defeat at the polls.

I think one of the most socially-beneficial accomplishments of EA was that it spawned dozens of young activists who went on to play large roles not only in the environmental movement but in other social change movements of the day: corporate reform, civil rights, economic justice, feminism, the rights of indigenous populations, animal rights, etc.

I was a friend and enthusiastic supporter of Environmental Action from the day it opened its doors in 1970 until the day it closed its doors in 1997. Down through those years, a great many worthy people passed through those doors — young, talented, passionate, dedicated, ingenious, and smart as whips. All that — plus — they had to be willing to work for a song.

Working as a community organizer, I interacted with many of these worthies in some way or other over many years. The following list is by no means a complete list of EA veterans. It's a list of EA veterans I *remember* interacting with — and it's a mighty big crowd.

On the 50th anniversary of Earth Day, I gladly bow in gratitude before them all.

Barbara Reid Alexander	Ruth Lampi
Bob Alvarez	Cathy Lerza
Leonard Arrow	Sam Love
Deborah Baldwin	Francesca Lyman
Dennis Bass	Diane MacEachern
Dan Becker	Alden Meyer
David Bryant	Phil Michael
Ruth Caplan	April Moore
Tom Chalkley	Rick Morgan
George Coling	Dick Munson
Claudia Comins	Carol Parker
Ana Crapsey	Gail Robinson
Gail Danker	Tony Roisman
Blake Early	Jan Schaeffer
Steve Haft	Doug Scott
Bryce Hamilton	Jeff Stansbery
Gail Harmon	Patricia Taylor
Peter Harnik	Mike Troutman
Sandra Jerabek	Frank Wallick
Richard John Kinane	Ruth Wallick
Craig Koralek	Marchant Wentworth
Ann Krumboltz	

IN MEMORIAM

What a melancholy task I set myself when I decided to compile a list of my collaborators from the 1960s and 1970s who have died. (And, alas, it's a *long* list.) Instead, however, I'm happy to report that fulfilling this task turned out to be a pleasure — reacquainting myself with these departed friends and allies.

Oh, how I wish I could wave a magic wand and bring all these old green pioneers back to life! God knows we could use them today. They sure as heck were movers and shakers when they were alive. They accomplished wonders — wonders from which we are still profiting.

Please join me in honoring the memory of these grand and glorious Green Pioneers.

Sammie Abdullah Abbott (1908-1990)

Sammie Abbott was one of the most cantankerous men I ever met, and the world is better for it. He was always feisty, always agitating against some perceived evil. "I'm a perpetually mad person," he was quoted as saying of himself.

Sammie was hauled before the House Un-American Activities Committee for his involvement in the peace movement and civil rights and ended up being fired from his job. By his own account, he was arrested about 40 times, the last in 1988 when protesting the eviction of renters in Takoma Park, Maryland, his hometown.

I met Sammie in the late 1960s when he gained notoriety by standing in front of bulldozers to stop construction of freeways in Washington, DC, my hometown. Most notably, these projects were:

- The Three Sisters Bridge over the Potomac, an expanse designed to carry cars and trucks over super-highways into downtown Washington where they would hook up with K Street; and

- The North-Central Freeway which was slated to connect a downtown "inner loop" with the I-495 Beltway north of the city. Ten lanes wide, the freeway would cut through black neighborhoods in northeast DC and would necessitate the demolition of thousands of homes.

In 1968, Sammie, working with the late Reggie Booker and the late Angela Rooney, two other amazingly effective neighborhood activists, formed the Emergency Committee on the Transportation Crisis (ECTC). Over the next few years, ECTC led more than 75 street protests, drawing support from black and white DC and Maryland residents whose communities were in the planned freeway's path.

(I'm proud to state that Glenn Pinder, my husband, and I were field soldiers in this campaign, marching as to war. At the time, in the press, we demonstrators were accused of throwing rocks at policemen, but I swear to you on a stack of Bibles that neither Glenn nor I have ever thrown a rock at anyone, not even each other.)

Finally, in 1971, these freeways were canceled and Congress, in its wisdom, re-allocated the highway construction funds to the building of DC's Metrorail system.

Looking back, Angela Rooney had an interesting take on this achievement. "When people fly into Washington, they look down and marvel at how pretty it is," she said. "Well, it wouldn't look that way if not for Sammie Abbott." Angela was right. Instead, what they'd see would be a jumble of concrete freeways.

Malcolm Baldwin (1940-2018)

While working at the Conservation Foundation in the mid-1960s, Malcolm convened the first national conference on environmental law and co-wrote and edited *Law and the Environment,* a book that helped guide the then-emerging field of environmental law. He was one of the founders of the Environmental Law Institute.

After Earth Day, I remember that Malcolm was instrumental in bringing the National Wildlife Federation into the environmental movement by getting them to oppose the numerous proposals then extant for new highway construction in national parks.

Leila (Lee) Botts (1928-2019)

Lee Botts was a pioneering and globally recognized American environmentalist who was for years the leader of efforts to protect and restore the Great Lakes. And she was one of the most exceptional women I have known and worked with. I admired her tremendously.

In the 1960s, Lee joined the Save the Dunes Council's campaign to protect the Indiana Dunes in northwest Indiana, which were a favorite haunt of her family. In 1966, that campaign succeeded with the creation of the Indiana Dunes National Lakeshore (now the Indiana Dunes National Park).

In 1968, Lee joined the staff of the Open Lands Project in Chicago (now Openlands), one of the city's first environmental organizations.

In 1970, she helped organize Earth Day in Chicago, a project in which she and I collaborated.

Lee founded the Lake Michigan Federation (now the Alliance for the Great Lakes). Under her leadership from 1971 to 1975, the new organization persuaded Mayor Richard J. Daley to have Chicago become the first Great Lakes city to ban phosphates in laundry detergents. The Federation led US advocacy for the first binational Great Lakes Water Quality Agreement (1972). It was a key advocate for the landmark federal Clean Water Act of 1972 and played a key role in persuading Congress to ban PCBs through the 1976 Toxic Substances Control Act. The organization has continued to grow in scope and influence and is now the Alliance for the Great Lakes.

In 1977, Lee was appointed by President Jimmy Carter to head the Great Lakes Basin Commission, a federal agency based in Ann Arbor, Michigan.

Lee Botts was a great teacher. For decades, she served as a mentor to many environmentalists in the Chicago area, northwest Indiana, and the Great Lakes region.

Stewart M. Brandborg (1925-2018)

Stewart Brandborg, known as "Brandy," came to Washington in the 1950s to work for the National Wildlife Federation and was soon recruited to the Wilderness Society. He led the Wilderness Society from 1956-1976, first on the Governing Council, then on the staff, and for 12 years as the executive director. During his tenure, more than 70 wilderness areas in 31 states were brought under the Wilderness Act's protection.

Brandy helped draft, and then advocate for passage, the landmark Wilderness Act of 1964 that set aside millions of acres of land for protection from human development. Since 1964, the National Wilderness Preservation System had expanded almost every year. It now includes 765 wilderness areas covering nearly 110 million acres in 44 states and Puerto Rico.

Joe Browder (1938-2016)

Joe Browder was called "the guardian of the Florida Everglades" in recognition of the valiant fight he began in 1961 to protect the natural wonder he loved so much. In the late 1960s, Joe led the successful opposition to the construction of a commercial airport on the western edge of the Everglades, about 50 miles west of Miami. The proposed Everglades Jetport would have been the world's largest airport, five times the size of John F. Kennedy International Airport in New York. Today that airport ain't there, thank goodness. Where it would have been is now the site of Everglades National Park. Thank you, Joe Browder!

David Burwell (1947-2017)

David Burwell's environmental legacy is an extraordinary one. He helped build a national movement to preserve green space and to provide options for alternative modes of transportation.

In the early 1980s, struggling railroads were abandoning 4,000 to 8,000 miles of rail line each year. The Rails-to-Trails Conservancy, which David founded in 1986 with Peter Harnik, built a national network to convert these unused railroad corridors to trails and parklands.

The Conservancy brought together walking, hiking, and cycling enthusiasts; railroad history buffs; representatives from environmental, conservation and parks groups; and alternative transportation advocates to preserve these abandoned rail corridors as nature and bicycle trails. These efforts have paid off in spades.

Today, the conservancy has helped build more than 2,000 trails on more than 22,000 miles of rail corridors in all 50 states and the District of Columbia.

Robert Cahn (1917-1997)

I met Bob Cahn when he was a writer-in-residence at the Conservation Foundation.

What an avid environmentalist he was! He was the environmental editor of the *Christian Science Monitor,* which in 1968 published a series of his stories titled *Will Success Spoil the National Parks?* The stories won the 1969 Pulitzer Prize for National Reporting. From 1970 to 1972, he served on the President's Council on Environmental Quality.

During the 1970s, Bob worked as field editor of *Audubon* magazine. He also wrote stories for *Reader's Digest, Smithsonian, World Monitor, TV Guide, Environment, Sierra,* and *Earth Work.*

Wilson Clark (1947-1983)

Author, *Energy for Survival: The Alternative to Extinction* (1974). Immediately after Earth Day in 1970, we organizers realized that we had to quickly acquire an understanding of energy problems and issues. Frankly, most of us didn't know beans about energy. Anti-pollution was our game, so we had a lot of catching up to do. Wilson Clark, bless his heart, was our great teacher, and his book became our bible on energy.

Wilson was also a director of the Environmental Policy Institute and a founder of the Environmental Policy Center.

Ruth Clusen (1922–2005)

An ardent environmentalist, Ruth was especially concerned with water quality. She served as President of the National League of Women Voters (1974-78) and then as Assistant Secretary for the Environment at the Energy Department (1978 to 1981).

Douglas Michael Costle (1939 –2019)

I met Doug Costle in the early 1970s when he was Commissioner of Environmental Protection for the state of Connecticut. I was hugely impressed by him from the moment we met — and for a very simple reason. Doug had hired as his assistant, Mary Ann Massey, who had been my assistant when I worked for the Conservation Foundation.

It was instantly clear to me that Doug had discovered, as I had, that inside this demure, self-effacing ex-nun there dwelt a sharp, tough Irish pol who could have taught "Boss" Tweed a thing or two. He was guided by her as I had been. Thus, a bond formed between Doug Costle and me.

In 1977, Doug Costle went on to become Administrator of the Environmental Protection Agency during the Carter administration. (Mary Ann worked for him there.) He couldn't have been more qualified for the post, since he had, in fact, been one of the architects who designed the agency.

After working for the Justice Department's civil rights division in the mid-1960s, Doug was named to a White House advisory council with the aim of reorganizing the executive branch. He wound up outlining the scope of an independent agency that would coordinate federal efforts to protect the environment and public health. This became the EPA, which President Nixon formally launched by executive order in December 1970.

As the new EPA Administrator, Doug determined to greatly strengthen the agency's scientific competence; and, within two months of taking office, he recruited 600 scientists and other professionals. After the Love Canal health crisis near Niagara Falls, NY, he worked to create the Superfund to decontaminate toxic waste sites.

Doug held the position of EPA Administrator until 1981. He served as dean of Vermont Law School from 1987 to 1991.

Sir Frank Fraser Darling (1903 –1979)

I met Sir Frank when we worked together at the Conservation Foundation in the late 1960s, and I was honored to meet him. He was a distinguished ecologist and ornithologist, an Englishman who'd been Knighted for his service to science.

Sir Frank had written three acclaimed academic works that described the social and breeding behavior of red deer, gulls, and grey seals: *A Herd of Red Deer, Bird Flocks and the Breeding Cycle,* and *A Naturalist on Rona.*

In scientific lingo of ecology, his name had been given to "the Fraser Darling effect," which he proposed in 1938. This describes the simultaneous and shortened breeding season that occurs in large colonies of birds. This synchronized and accelerated breeding leads to a greater chance of survival for each individual offspring.

I was surprised, but gratified, that Sir Frank took an active interest in the community organizing I was doing. After all, he was a world-famous scientist, and I was just a grassroots activist whose name had been given to no effect whatsoever.

But Sir Frank was a naturalist/philosopher, with an original turn of mind and great intellectual curiosity. He *really wanted to know* what a community organizer did, and he took some pains to support my work at the foundation, which I'm grateful for to this day.

Henry Diamond (1932-2016)

Henry Diamond was a passionate advocate of environmental protection who got into the game early. A lawyer, his lengthy career contributed greatly to the development of environmental law in the United States. He is a particular hero of mine.

Following his graduation from Georgetown's National Law Center, Henry worked for Outdoor Recreation Resources Review Commission, established by President Kennedy in 1962. The Commission, chaired by Laurance S. Rockefeller, issued a seminal report, edited by Henry, that led to the creation of the Land and Water Conservation Fund, the Wilderness Act, and a national system of wild and scenic rivers. Not a bad start, huh?

I met Henry when he was Executive Director of the 1965 White House Conference on Natural Beauty. I was then working for the Interior Department's Bureau of Outdoor Recreation — specifically on the staff that had been assigned to develop and support Ladybird Johnson's beautification program — the First Lady's pet project.

In this position, I worked closely with Sharon Francis, Mrs. Johnson's assistant for beautification. Sharon, like me, was enthralled by the (then newly minted) ecological worldview; and, like me, she was zealously planting the idea every chance she got. She is a particular heroine of mine.

I think it was Sharon who arranged for my appointment to serve as Henry's assistant at the White House Conference, where I was responsible for doing whatever needed doing, no matter how trivial or laborious. What a splendid education!

The White House Conference brought together an astonishing array of conservationists, government officials, business people, labor leaders, and civic leaders of many kinds. The conference's aim was to secure restrictions on billboards and automobile junkyards, to encourage flower and tree-planting programs, and to promote highways adjoined with wildflowers and natural vegetation such as grassland. Many of these ideas were authorized by the Highway Beautification Act, which became law in October 1965.

The Governors of 35 states subsequently convened statewide natural beauty conferences. A wave of citizen action followed, dedicated to neighborhood improvement, protection of the countryside, and expanded preservation of historic sites and areas.

The immense *profundity* of Mrs. Johnson's "beautification" campaign often escaped notice back then. But Henry Diamond perceived it, Sharon Francis perceived it, and I perceived it. And, of course, Mrs. Johnson perceived it, perhaps better than anyone.

In her diary, she compared beautification to "picking up a tangled skein of wool. All the threads are interwoven — recreation and pollution and mental health, and the crime rate, and rapid transit, and highway beautification, and the war on poverty, and parks — national, state and local. It is hard to hitch the conversation into one straight line, because everything leads to something else."

Hey, imagine that! Ladybird was articulating the First Law of Ecology years before Professor Barry Commoner famously established it in his book, *The Closing Circle*, published in 1971.

Looking back, I regard Mrs. Johnson's natural beauty campaign as a predecessor to the environmental movement which was to explode later, on Earth Day in 1970, and then engulf the world at large.

It was on April 22, 1970 — Earth Day — that Henry was appointed as the first Commissioner of the New York Department of Environmental Conservation by Gov. Nelson Rockefeller. As Commissioner, Henry pressed for legislative and statewide voter approval of the 1972 Environmental Quality Bond Act. He led a 533-mile bicycle ride across New York State to promote the $1.2 billion bond issue, which provided for water and air pollution control and land acquisition.

Later, in 1974, Diamond was a co-founder of a major environmental and land use law firm, now Beveridge and Diamond, where he introduced corporate clients to the new world of federal and state regulation, while continuing to contribute his time to a host of good causes to support environmental conservation and education. It's been said that the firm's origins and evolution parallel the development of US environmental and natural resource regulation.

In 2015, Henry Diamond received the Environmental Law Institute's lifetime achievement award recognizing him as an "environmental statesman" who shaped a new field of law.

William J. Duddleson (1921-2014)

In the mid-1960s, Bill Duddleson and I worked together at the Interior Department's Bureau of Outdoor Recreation on Ladybird's beautification project. Then, he left to join the staff at the Conservation Foundation. In 1968, I followed him there.

Environmentalists tend to be people who are strongly committed to the cause. Boy, oh, boy, that was sure true of Bill Duddleson! And his heart was dedicated to his home state of California.

In 1958, he was working at the *Santa Rosa Press-Democrat* as a reporter when Clem Miller (Dem.) was elected congressman from the 1st District in California. Miller asked Bill to become his legislative assistant. The Congressman wanted Bill's help in turning a 35,000-acre portion of the Marin County shoreline into a national park, saving it from development and making it available to the public. The pair worked hard at this and — lo and behold — they succeeded in Miller's first term! (Miller served but one term. He was killed in an airplane crash in 1962.)

In 1962, President Kennedy signed the Point Reyes National Seashore bill into law. In 1966, Ladybird Johnson presided over the dedication ceremony for Point Reyes National Seashore.

Bill considered his beloved Point Reyes, his greatest accomplishment; and, with Point Reyes, he left a legacy for future generations.

Helen Fenske (1922-2007)

Helen Fenske was called "the environmental lioness of New Jersey." She led a campaign in the 1960s to block New York's Port Authority's plan to build an international jetport in New Jersey's Great Swamp, located in Morris County. The plan would have filled in the swamp in order to construct four 10,000-foot runways. But instead, thanks to Helen's campaign, the Great Swamp became a National Wildlife Refuge in 1964. It was said of Helen that "nobody had ever defeated the Port Authority before."

Later, she served as Assistant Commissioner of the New Jersey Department of Environmental Protection.

Richard Grossman (1943-2011)

In the early 1970s, Hazel Henderson, Peter Harnik, and I co-founded Environmentalists for Full Employment (EFFE), a group that worked to reconcile the interests of environmental activists and union members. We hired a young community organizer named Richard Grossman to run it. The job fitted his passion. Richard was an ardent opponent of corporations' influence on American politics.

He was the author of *Defying Corporations, Defining Democracy: A Book of History & Strategy* and *Taking Care of Business: Citizenship and the Charter of Incorporation.*

Virginia Harbin (dates unavailable)

Virginia Harbin was a founding member of The Georgia Conservancy and its administrator for many years. In the late 1960s, I worked closely with Virginia and other Conservancy leaders, Lucy

Cabot Smethurst, Barbara Blum, and Merle Lefkoff, to organize the environmental movement in the state. Then in 1970, we teamed up to organize Earth Day in Georgia. What a fabulous bunch of women leaders — all smart as whips and astute politicians to boot. Virginia, demure and determined, was our commander-in-chief who quietly pulled strings to pull off political miracles.

To date, the Georgia Conservancy has protected more than 338,000 acres in the state, while also safeguarding the state's rivers and coast.

John 'Jay' Harris IV (1928-2009)

Jay Harris was called "a venture capitalist for the environment."

Like his friend and collaborator, John Hunting, Jay was not only a dedicated philanthropist but a daring and innovative one. I was but one of the oddball grassroots activists that he laid a bet on. Like me, Jay was a "small is beautiful" freak, and he put his money where his mouth was. He grasped the unusual significance of my political outreach to small business and generously funded it.

Jay called his foundation the Changing Horizons Fund because he believed that our priorities must always be changing to meet new challenges.

The Changing Horizons Fund provided grants to organizations such as the Center for Food Safety and the National Coalition Against the Misuse of Pesticides. He also aided the Sierra Club, Planned Parenthood of Southeastern Pennsylvania, and Zero Population Growth.

Jay saw the big picture in big ways. He was a founder of the US Association for the Club of Rome and chaired (and funded) the organization for many years. The Club of Rome, founded in 1968, is a futurist, nonprofit nongovernmental organization that serves as an international think tank on global issues.

The Club's first report, *The Limits to Growth*, was published in 1972. It was based on computer simulations which suggested that economic growth could not continue indefinitely because of resource depletion. The report sold 30 million copies in more than 30 languages, making it the best-selling environmental book in history.

Gladwin Hill (1914-1997)

In the early days of the environmental movement, we had no better friend than Gladwin Hill. He was our journalistic touchstone. Gladwin was with *The New York Times* for 44 years. He pioneered environmental reporting. From 1969 until his retirement in 1979, he served as national environmental correspondent for *The Times*, the first reporter at the newspaper and one of the first in the nation to cover the environment full time. He travelled the country to report on air and water pollution, issues that had only just begun to register in the national consciousness.

Gladwin wrote *Madman in a Lifeboat: Issues of the Environmental Crisis* (1973).

M. Carl Holman (1919-1988)

Carl Holman was a nationally prominent and highly respected American civil rights leader. He was President of the National Urban Coalition (1971–88) and served as Co-Chair, National Conference on Public Transportation, sponsored by the Conservation Foundation and the National Urban Coalition (1972). This conference, which I organized, convened representatives of virtually every group in the country with an interest in the furtherance of public transportation. Carl did a fabulous job of bringing in minority group leaders.

William C. Holmberg (1928-2016)

Bill Holmberg, a retired Marine Corps lieutenant colonel who received the Navy Cross for his actions on a Korean battlefield, later spent decades as a passionate advocate on Capitol Hill for renewable energy and environmental causes.

What a charismatic guy he was! Always brimming with energy! It was like nothing could stop him.

Bill brought the discipline and devotion learned during his military training to bear in the field of renewable energy (specifically biomass fuels from cellulose). He was tireless and a true original devoted to the health of the earth and future generations.

After his military retirement in 1970, Bill spent years directing the Energy Department's Office of Alcohol Fuel, where he championed ethanol as a sustainable, alternative energy source. In 2001, Sen. Tom Daschle (D-S.D.), then majority leader, praised Bill Holmberg not only as "a war hero but an indefatigable champion of the environment."

Bill understood the importance of bioenergy in our nation's future. He led the way in bioenergy, both in US government agencies and with Congress; and he actively educated environmentalists, farm groups, policymakers, journalists on sustainable energy and agriculture.

Sydney Howe (1929-1996)

I met Syd Howe when I joined the Conservation Foundation in 1968. He became the foundation's president in 1969 and remained in the post until 1973.

Syd was an early fighter for clean soil, water, and air; but what was distinctive about him was this: he was one of the first environmentalists to insist that a balance must be struck between the needs of the environment and the needs of the poor. He argued that poor people living in the cities suffered the most from air, water, and noise pollution and thus deserved special attention.

Syd was dead serious about this objective. He couldn't have been more earnest. He spent much of his career toiling on behalf of (what is now called) environmental justice. It was an uphill climb all the way and remains so to this day.

In 1976, Syd founded the Urban Environment Foundation and served as its Executive Director. Its specific focus was to obtain greater minority participation in jobs related to the environment.

Robert S. Hutchings (1914-2002)

My first job out of college landed me not in *hot* but *dirty* water.

From 1959 to 1965, I worked for the Division of Water Supply and Pollution Control, US Public Health Service, located then in the old Department of Health, Education, and Welfare. (I didn't know it then; but, for someone fated to devote his life's work to environmental protection, it was just the place to be. I was in on the ground floor of the environmental movement before there was a ground floor.)

Bob Hutchings — my first boss and the best boss I ever had — was Chief of the Information Branch, and I was his assistant. "Hutch" was a sophisticated New Yorker, who had left a long career at J. Walter Thompson, the public relations firm, to start a new career in mid-life in public service.

I owe much to him. For one thing, he taught me to write with both verve and restraint, no mean trick.

In 1962, "Hutch" organized the first ever Advertising Council public service campaign that can be labelled "environmental." (The Ad Council had been doing the Smokey the Bear Wildfire Prevention campaign since 1944, but that would be considered a *conservation* campaign, not an *environmental* one.)

The clean water campaign was a series of public service announcements hosted by John Charles Daly, a broadcast journalist famous in those days as the host and moderator of the CBS television panel show, *What's My Line?*

In the early 1960s, water pollution was not widely recognized as a problem. But, of course, later in the decade as the environmental revolution exploded, water pollution control was propelled to the top of the nation's agenda. In part, this was thanks to the Ad Council campaign we launched. While lauding this achievement, I must enthusiastically cite the first-rate work done by other team members, Jack Hardesty, Mort Lebow, and Adrian "Duke" Sybor.

Having helped put the kibosh on dirty water, Hutchings spent the rest of his career putting the kibosh on tobacco. From 1967 to 1989, he was the Director of Information and Public Education for the National Clearinghouse on Smoking and Health.

Marcey Jaskulski (1926 -2015)

Marcey's passion was to protect the environment for future generations by securing clean air and water for Milwaukee County and the state of Wisconsin. She was the first president of the South Eastern Wisconsin Coalition for Clean Air, one of the coalitions that I organized when I was working for the Conservation Foundation. Marcey also served as president of the Milwaukee River Restoration Counsel. She was appointed by the governor to the Wisconsin Air Pollution Advisory Council and by Senator Edward Kennedy to the task force to promote citizen participation in the Congressional Office of Technology Assessment.

Jeanne Malchon (1923-2017)

Florida State Senator Jeanne Malchon sponsored the 1985 Florida Clean Indoor Air Act which outlawed smoking in a variety of commonly shared places, such as airline terminals.

She was a wonder to behold, a shrewd and successful politician in real world terms, while never relaxing for a moment her firm commitment to idealistic goals.

I met Jeanne in the 1970s when she was President of the American Lung Association. We worked together to make the association and its many state and local affiliates active participants in the environmental movement, an effort which paid off in spades. Public health became a major component of environmentalism, as important as pollution control, wilderness protection, or any other factor.

In 1977, President Carter appointed Jeanne to the National Clean Air Commission.

Anthony 'Tony' Mazzocchi (1926-2002)

Tony Mazzocchi, a vice president of the Oil, Chemical and Atomic Workers International Union, was called the "Rachel Carson of the American workplace" and for good reason. In 1962, Tony read Carson's book, *Silent Spring*. He reasoned that if small doses of the chemicals described in the book caused environmental harm, the workers who received large doses in manufacturing plants must be in medical danger.

Mobilized by this realization, Tony began seeking support in the environmental movement for worker health and safety. He encouraged the labor movement to support the environmental movement, and vice versa. His efforts paid off in the passage of major federal legislation to protect industrial workers from environmental harm.

Tony chaired the first Earth Day rally in New York City on April 22, 1970.

The Steelworkers' Tony Mazzocchi Center for Health, Safety and Environmental Education in Pittsburgh, PA, is dedicated to him. The

Center aims to prevent work-related injuries and illness by providing health, safety, and environmental training to local union officers, to union health and safety activists, and directly to workers themselves.

W. Rice Odell (1928-2015)

Rice Odell possesses a distinctive claim to fame in the history of environmentalism. He wrote and edited The Conservation Foundation newsletter during the 1960s and 70s, a series which I rank amongst the founding documents of the environmental revolution.

Remember, back in those days, the environmental take on things came as news to most people. It was a new way of looking, not just at nature but at humankind in the embrace of nature. It had to be explained — *interpreted,* really— in accessible and palatable form. A tough assignment — and Rice was just the guy to take it on.

He was a tireless researcher, a probing intellect who took delight in the discovery of new ideas. Rice was very even-handed and fair-minded. Objections to the environmental stance on things were trotted out and fully aired. The pieces he wrote were never one-sided. He wouldn't have stooped to that in a hundred years.

As a writer, Rice aimed to make things clear and sharp, but also short and sweet. The newsletter format suited him to a T — just long enough but not too long, more than a newspaper column, but less than a book.

Over the years, Rice addressed all the fundamental issue of environmentalism, covering them one by one, issue by issue. As a reader, when I had finished one of his newsletters, I felt I'd acquired a sufficient mastery of the issue to engage in political discourses about it or even debates.

Rice, old boy, you were one in a million!

Rice Odell was also the author of several books, including *The Saving of San Francisco Bay* (1972) and *Environmental Awakening* (1980).

In 1997, Rice co-authored with Barbara Rodes, *A Dictionary of Environmental Quotations. This* book contains more than 3,700 quotations in 143 categories—from Acid Rain to Zoos—a comprehensive collection of wise and witty observations about our natural environment.

(I'm pleased to be one of the persons quoted: "If you don't like diversity, drop dead!" — Byron Kennard)

Gunnar A. Peterson (1915-1976)

Gunnar was a principal organizer of the environmental movement in the Chicago region. He and Lee Botts worked together closely — what a team they made! In 1970, they co-founded the Lake Michigan Federation. They were my always-reliable Chicago connections in the heady days of the 1960s and 1970s.

Gunner was Executive Director of the Open Lands Project; and, in the early 1960s, he led the effort to preserve Goose Lake Prairie. The site's preservation was finally authorized in 1968. Goose Lake, which consists of over 1,700 acres of prairie and marsh communities, is the largest remnant of prairie left in Illinois.

The Visitor Center at Goose Lake Prairie, opened in 1977, is named in Gunner's honor.

Alex Radin (1922-2014)

Alex was the face of the public power industry in Washington, DC, for more than three decades and a longtime, savvy supporter of the environmental movement.

He was chief executive officer of the American Public Power Association (APPA), a national trade association representing more than 2,000 not-for-profit power utilities.

Under his leadership, APPA became the first electric utility association to call for federal legislation to address the consequences of acid rain and to advocate for environmental regulation.

Alex was one of the founders of the Consumer Federation of America.

Angela L. Rooney (1919-2016)

In Washington, DC, Angela Rooney was locally famous as a co-founder of the Emergency Committee on the Transportation Crisis, which waged a successful campaign to halt construction of the North Central Freeway in Washington, DC, and the Three Sisters Bridge over the Potomac River.

Without Angela, Washington, DC, would have Interstate 95 running through the middle of the city. If Sammie Abbott was the fiercely beating heart of the anti-freeway movement, Angela was its pure soul, inspiring many others (me included) to continue the struggle when the going got rough (which it frequently did).

However, here I celebrate Angela Rooney for doing things other than stopping freeways, important as stopping them was. To me, Angela *was emblematic of what a neighborhood activist should be.*

Listen, it's perfectly fine to weep and wail over the fate of the whole planet; I've spent a lifetime doing it. But, environmentally speaking, action at the neighborhood scale is where it all begins.

Neighborhoods need defending, and residents often learn — to their surprise and sorrow — that they can't rely on local politicians and city officials to do the defending. Often, local politicians and city officials are the *foes*.

Thankfully, Mother Nature, in her bountiful wisdom, has seen to it that some local residents are programmed to become the needed defenders. These are *private* citizens who become *public* citizens. I think Mother Nature must have crafted Angela Rooney as the model.

Angela was perhaps the single most effective *neighborhood* activist I ever encountered in my sixty years as a community organizer. She lived in Northeast Washington, DC., in Brookland, a neighborhood of tree-lined streets filled with older homes.

Her eagle eye never missed a thing going on in Brookland. She was involved with historic preservation, with local arts and artists, and the quality of education. If libraries had to be persuaded to stay open in the evenings so working people could use them, she was there, making sure it happened. If the local park wasn't being well maintained, she'd get after the city.

If the trash wasn't being picked up regularly, she knew just who in the Sanitation Department to call to complain about it. She worked non-stop. It was a full-time job but, of course, non-salaried. Her reward, I think, was that Brookland remained a quiet, pleasant, comfortable place for people to live and raise families. Today, it still is.

Jack Sheehan (1926-2017)

Jack Sheehan, in the words of one of his colleagues, was "one of the truly great labor activists." That's certainly the impression of him that I formed.

Jack spent his career – from 1959 to 1996 – as Legislative Director of the United Steelworkers of America (USWA).

Jack essentially made the environment a union issue in the 1960s. Through Jack, the USWA advocated passionately for every major environmental bill and persuaded the USWA to support the Clean Air Act of 1963. Under Jack's leadership, the USWA held its first union-wide environmental conference in 1969.

With Jack's driving support, the USWA became a founding member of the National Clean Air Coalition.

Jack was a long-time national board member and later honorary trustee of the Natural Resources Defense Council (NRDC) and served as well on the advisory board of the Environmental and Energy Study Institute (EESI) in Washington.

I think Jack was prescient in a way about the global nature of environmental issues. Here's why: in 1991, testifying before the Senate Finance Committee, he stated that, "given current warming trends, environmental policy can no longer be exclusively national in scope."

Hey, I repeat, *that was in 1991*. If only his counsel had been heeded back then!

James Noel Smith (1937-2011)

Jim Smith and I worked together at the Conservation Foundation in the late 1960s and early 1970s, both of us lucky enough to be in the right place at the right time.

In 1969, when Senator Gaylord Nelson got a resolution through Congress calling for a National Teach-In on the Environment, he asked the Foundation to help get the show off the ground, and we jumped right in. (The foundation gave the fledging Teach-In organization $75,000 to get started.)

Jim Smith was appointed to head this effort. In my book, Jim's claim to fame is that he chose the date for Earth Day — April 22, 1970, a date that lives in history.

Since the project at that early stage (not yet Earth Day) was modeled on the teach-ins used successfully by Vietnam War protesters to spread their message and generate support on US college campuses, Jim focused on dates that fell between spring break and final exams so that a majority of college students would be able to participate. He gave much time and thought to this process.

Then he zeroed in on Wednesday, April 22.

Of course, there was no Internet in those days to research things like this, but Jim had chosen a date — totally unbeknownst to him (or any of us) — that just happened to be the hundredth anniversary of the birth of Vladimir Lenin.

Oh, dear! Soon, this set off a rumor in the nether world of right-wing nuttiness that Earth Day was a secret conspiracy, more red than green, and more about communism than conservation.

Unbelievably, this tired, old conspiracy theory circulates to this day. Jim and I must have laughed about this a hundred times over the years.

Russell E. Train (1920-2012)

Russ Train was President of the Conservation Foundation from 1965 to 1969. It was he who, in 1968, made the remarkably astute decision to hire me to work as a community organizer for the foundation. But — grateful as I am — I'm duty bound to declare that hiring me was by no means his most illustrious distinction. He did much greater things.

Russ served as Under Secretary of the Department of the Interior (1969 to 1970). Then he became Administrator of the EPA under Presidents Nixon and Ford, before becoming president and chairman of World Wildlife Fund from 1978 to 1990.

That's all very impressive, but I suspect that what gave Russ his greatest pride and joy was the work he did to protect African wildlife. In the 1950s, while on safari there, he fell in love with Africa. Later he credited this safari with awakening his environmentalism.

In 1961, Russ co-founded the African Wildlife Leadership Foundation in order to build the capacity of Africans to steward their own natural resources. The organization is now known as the African Wildlife Foundation (AWF).

AWF helped found the College of African Wildlife Management in Mweka, Tanzania, which began formal training of African wildlife managers in 1963. Among other things, the college prepares students to work in the national parks and nature reserves of Africa.

Since its inception, AWF has helped train hundreds of African wildlife managers and has succeeded in reducing the poaching of tigers, lions, elephants, and other African primates.

David Zwick (1947-2018)

David Zwick was a student at Harvard Law School in the early 1970s when he joined a group of attorneys working with consumer activist Ralph Nader. He wound up heading a groundbreaking study of the nation's water pollution. David's research and organizing spurred passage of the Clean Water Act of 1972 and the Safe Drinking Water Act of 1974. He was the longtime president of Clean Water Action, a national organization he founded in 1972.

Today, our water is more fishable, swimmable, and drinkable because of David Zwick's work.

Appendix #2

The Environmental Justice Movement

As the environmental revolution came to the fore with its emphasis on our needs for clean air and water, it became clear to some that we humans had done a pretty good job of dumping and perpetuating all our environmental messes on those with the least power in society, the poor and minorities.

Much evidence was developed demonstrating these populations were being ignored in the growing effort to improve and maintain a clean and healthful environment. With this knowledge in hand, the actions of a number of individuals and organizations to address this situation grew into the environmental justice movement.

The Natural Resources Defense Council (NRDC), now led by former EPA Administrator Gina McCarthy, has made advocacy of environmental justice a priority. The organization's statement on the subject is worth quoting:

"Championed primarily by African-Americans, Latinos, Asians and Pacific Islanders, and Native Americans, the environmental justice movement addresses a statistical fact: People who live, work, and play in America's most polluted environments are commonly people of color and the poor. Environmental justice advocates have shown that this is no accident. Communities of color, which are often also low-income, are routinely targeted to host facilities that have negative environmental impacts—say, a landfill, dirty industrial plant, or truck depot. The statistics provide clear evidence of what the movement rightly calls *environmental racism*. Communities of color have been battling this injustice for decades."

Government and governmental institutions became involved in these issues. The new Council on Environmental Quality devoted a chapter in the 1971 annual report to the Inner-City Environment. In 1990, a group of advocates, led by Bunyan Bryant with the University of Michigan, visited with then EPA Administrator William Reilly to make their case. He directed EPA's policy office to review what was known and from this review created the Office of Environmental Equity, naming a senior staff member Clarice Gaylord to lead the effort. The office was renamed Environmental justice by Reilly's successor Carol Browner.

EPA has defined environmental justice as:

"[T]he fair treatment and meaningful involvement of all people regardless of race, ethnicity, income, national origin, or educational level with respect to the development, implementation and enforcement of environmental laws, regulations and policies. Fair treatment means that no population, due to policy or economic disempowerment, is forced to bear a disproportionate burden of the negative human health or environmental impacts of pollution or other environmental consequences resulting from industrial, municipal, and commercial operations or the execution of federal, state, local, and tribal programs and policies."

I personally have been only an observer of the efforts to bring the benefits of a clean environment to all. But with the theme of this book, it became clear to me that to neglect mention of this aspect of what has been wrought by "environmentalism" (a word used in the ecological sense only since the 1960's) would be a grave error. Since I have emphasized my belief that real and lasting change is brought about by *countless uncoordinated acts by countless uncoordinated actors,* but my conceit is an attempt to count some of those, I am including a list of some principal players in this environmental justice movement. The struggles and accomplishments of many are indeed of imposing importance.

Mustafa Santiago Ali, vice president, environmental justice, climate and community revitalization at the National Wildlife Federation. Formerly worked at the EPA for 24 years, where he was senior adviser and assistant associate administrator for environmental justice — an office he helped found in 1992 during the first Bush administration.

Bunyan Bryant, An emeritus professor with a 40-year career at the University of Michigan's School of Natural Resources and Environment, he was instrumental in establishing the school's Environmental Justice Program, focusing on the differential impact of environmental contaminants on people of color and low-income communities He was co-organizer of the 1990 Conference on Race and the Incidence of Environmental Hazards. In 1991, he was on the Advisory Committee of the First National People of Color Environmental Leadership Summit. He was a member of the EPA's National Environmental Justice Advisory Council. Bryant was a part of a movement that was responsible for President Clinton's signing of the Environmental Justice Executive Order 12898.

Dr. Robert Bullard, known as the father of environmental justice. He started working on environment and race issues in 1978 when he was collecting landfill data for a landmark civil rights lawsuit.

Majora Carter, founded and led the non-profit environmental justice solutions corporation Sustainable South Bronx from 2001 onward.

Cesar Chavez organized Latino farm in the early 1960s fight for workplace rights, including protection from harmful pesticides in the farm fields of California's San Joaquin valley.

Reverend Ben Chavis, Reverend Joseph Lowery, and **Reverend Leon White** — veterans of the civil rights movement — have taken the lead is fostering the environmental justice movement.

Bernadette Demientieff, executive director of the Gwich'in Steering Committee, which was formed in 1988 in response to proposed oil drilling on the coastal plain of the Arctic National Wildlife Refuge, an area known to the Gwich'in as the Sacred Place Where Life Begins.

Lisa DeVille, a member of the Three Affiliated Tribes on the Fort Berthold Reservation in North Dakota and serves as president of Fort Berthold Protectors of Water and Earth Rights, a grassroots organization fighting pollution.

Walter Fauntroy, District of Columbia Congressional Delegate and a chair of the Congressional Black Caucus.

Tom Goldtooth and his son **Dallas,** longtime activists on environmental issues and how they affect Native communities.

Antonio González, as leader of the Southwest Voter Registration Education Project was one of the first leaders of a national Latino-issues organization to address environment concerns directly.

Princess Daazhraii Johnson, Founding member, Fairbanks Climate Action Coalition. For more than 30 years, has been fighting to protect the Arctic National Wildlife Refuge from oil development that threatens the porcupine caribou, on which her tribe depends for survival.

Charles Lee, Director of Research, United Church of Christ's Commission for Racial Justice.

Vernice Miller-Travis, an early NRDC director of environmental justice.

Paul Mohai, professor at University of Michigan, a major contributor to the growing body of quantitative research examining disproportionate environmental burdens and their impacts on low income and people of color communities. He is also a member of the Advisory Board of the Global Environmental Justice Movement Project (ENVJUSTICE) which is documenting and mapping environmental justice conflicts around the world.

Richard Moore and ***Jeanne Gauna***, Co-Directors, Southwest Organizing Project, initiated a letter in 1990, signed by several environmental justice leaders, to the "Big 10" environmental groups, accusing them of racial bias in policy development, hiring, and the makeup of their boards, and challenging them to address toxic contamination in the communities and workplaces of people of color and the poor.

Kandi Mossett-White, the native energy and climate campaign coordinator at Indigenous Environmental Network.

Irma Munoz, founder and director of Mujeres de la Tierra, an organization that inspires women and their children to take leadership roles in their communities by identifying solutions to environmental problems.

Juan Parras, founder of Texas Environmental Justice Advocacy Services, a grassroots organization aimed at improving air quality and environmental health for the Lone Star State's most heavily polluted communities.

Lucy Ramos, one of the founders of Mothers of East L.A. started in 1986, as a group of Latina mothers under the guidance of Monsignor John Moretta, originally organized to stop the siting of a prison in the East Los Angeles community, then turned its attention to opposing a hazardous waste incinerator and has subsequently taken on other local environmental and social issues.

Norma Ramos, her work through West Harlem Environmental Action, Inc. (WE-ACT) connects health, safety, land use, and jobs.

Roger Rivera, president of the National Hispanic Environmental Council; engaged in the first efforts to organize Latinos to be part of solutions related to global warming, and to ensure that those solutions are equitable to all members of society.

Beverly L. Wright, environmental justice scholar and advocate, author, civic leader and professor of Sociology, is the founder and executive director of the Deep South Center for Environmental Justice.

Elizabeth Yeampierre, leads UPROSE, Brooklyn's oldest Latino community-based organization. She is a national leader on climate justice who advocates for sustainable development and was the first Latina chair of the EPA's National Environmental Justice Advisory Council.

Index

A

Abbey, Edward 24
Abbott, Sammie 224-226, 244
Alderson, George ix, 149, 160-161
Alexander, Barbara Reid 48, 149, 161, 221, 223
Ali, Mustafa Santiago 251
Allen, Maureen 118
Allen, Peter 118
Alvarez, Bob 223
Amazon rainforest 12, 44, 120
American Lung Association 50, 180, 241
Amon, Larry 161-162
Amrine, Eric 221
Anderson, Helen 155
Anthony, Carl Sferrazza x, 149
Apollo 17 astronaut photo 23
Arrow, Leonard 223
Attenborough, Sir David 8-9
Atwood, Margaret 24

B

Bald eagle 2, 116
Baldwin, Deborah 223
Baldwin, Malcolm 226
Ballard, J.G. 24
Bass, Dennis 223
BBC *Blue Planet II* 8-9, 46
Becker, Dan 223
Binder, Gordon iv, 148, 149, 150, 162-164
BioScience 12
Blackwelder, Brent 164-165
Blake, Lucy 165-166
Bogan, Walter 166

Bogus, Carl T.   154
Booker, Reggie   225
Bossong, Ken   166-167
Boy Scouts   50, 180, 205
Botts, Leila (Lee)   226-227, 243
Boyle, T.C.   24
Brandborg, Stewart M.   227
Browder, Joe   228
Brown, Joan Martin   150, 167-168, 177
Brown, Lester   168-169
Bryant, Bunyan   251
Bryant, David   223
Bullard, Dr. Robert   252
Burke, Edmund   73-80, 96-99, 102-103, 124, 130, 139-140, 151-154
Burrell, Charlie   118
Burwell, David   179, 228
Butler, Simon   56

C

Cahn, Robert   229
California redwood forest   120
Caplan, Ruth   223
Carson, Rachel   11-12, 24, 174, 191, 241
Carter, Majora   252
CFCs   2
Center for Small Business and the Environment   146, 154, 157-158
centralists   155
Chalkley, Tom   223
Chavez, Cesar   252
Chavis, Reverend Ben   252
cheetah   10, 44
Cherry, Lynne   169
Chile   117
chimpanzee   9-10
chipmunks   9
Church, Jeff   150
Churchill, Winston   134
Clark, Wilson   229
Clean Air Act   2, 28-29, 206, 246

Clean Air for Milwaukee 50, 240
Clean Water Act 28-29, 227, 248
Clevey, Mark H. 156
climate change iv, vii, 2, 4-5, 13, 16, 20-22, 24-26, 31-34, 40, 47, 56, 75, 93, 105, 106, 113, 122, 132-134, 143-144, 146, 158, 169, 190, 199, 203-205
The Closing Circle 55-56, 233
Clusen, Ruth 229
cognitive dissonance 151
Coling, George 221, 223
Comins, Claudia 223
Commoner, Barry 55-57, 213, 233
community organizing vii, 1, 48, 49, 58, 146, 148
connectedness 43, 97, 108
Conrad, Kent 221
Conservation Foundation 49, 146, 161, 162, 163, 180, 205, 207, 208, 226, 229, 230, 231, 234, 237, 238, 240, 242, 246, 247
conservatives iii, 81, 85, 89, 99-103, 122-129, 138-142, 152-153
Costle, Douglas Michael 167, 177, 230-231
Cotton, Stephen 221
Crapsey, Ana 223
creative destruction 37, 81-85, 140
Crosby, Mark 149, 150, 178

D

Dalsemer, Dick 221
Danker, Gail 223
Darling, Sir Frank Fraser 231
Day, Molly Brogan 155
DDT 2
deforestation 12, 106, 193
Demientieff, Bernadette 252
DeVille, Lisa 252
Diamond, Henry 176, 231-234
The Discovery Channel 26, 46
Drayton, William A. 170-171
Duddleson, William J. 234-235
Dunlap, Louise 171-172

E

Early, Blake 223
Earth Day 1, 6, 24-26, 28-31, 39-40, 45-48, 51, 53, 60-61, 65, 67, 70-71, 74, 140-141, 143, 146, 179-180, 183, 188, 194-195, 221-223, 233, 247
eco-fiction 24
ecological worldview 53-57, 63-72, 131, 137, 151, 175, 232
Edey, Marion 172-173
Edwards Dam 115-116
energy efficiency 18, 82-83, 127, 191, 196
Einstein, Albert 107, 138
Emerson, Ralph Waldo 52, 107
emission reductions 2, 18, 21, 138, 171
Endangered Species 2, 4, 12, 24, 29, 193, 195
entrepreneurs iv, vi, 19, 37, 76, 86, 92, 101, 130, 139, 146, 154, 157, 170-171, 214-215
environmental
  education 17-18, 166, 199
  justice movement 2, 104, 131, 139, 239, 249-254
  movement iii, iv, v, vii, ix, 31, 51, 146, 159, 160, 168, 183, 186, 195, 197, 204, 222, 226, 233, 237, 241, 243
  protection 2, 17, 19, 23-25, 28-29, 51, 63, 68, 75, 89, 91, 104, 130, 137, 139, 142, 143, 146, 222
  revolution 1-5, 14-18, 24, 26, 45, 57, 58, 60-62, 64, 68, 70, 130-133, 136-144, 208, 214, 242, 249
EPA 2, 163-164, 167-168, 170-171, 177-178, 183, 202, 206, 230, 247-248, 249-251, 254
equilibrium 99-100, 102-103
Evans, Brock 4-5, 149, 173-174

F

Farha, Ed 150
Fauntroy, Walter 252
Fenske, Helen 235
First Law of Ecology 54-57, 97, 131, 233
food chain 2
fossil fuels 13, 19, 30, 32, 56, 82, 84, 127, 128-129, 144, 166, 204, 211
France 69, 115
Francis, Sharon 150, 174-177, 232-233

Frenkil, David   150
freshwater tables   12

G

Garling, Andrew   221
Gauna, Jeanne   253
gay   25, 36, 152, 153
Generation X   131, 143-144
Generation Y   47, 131, 143-144
Generation Z   40, 47, 131, 134, 143-144
Girl Scouts   50, 180
Goldtooth, Dallas   252
Goldtooth, Tom   252
Gonzalez, Antonio   252
GreenBiz   7
green
   buildings   5, 20, 135, 138
   business   18-21, 76, 130, 154, 158
   communities   5
   neighborhoods   5
greenhouse gas emissions   2, 40-41, 82, 138, 193, 196, 203
Grossman, Richard   235

H

Haft, Steve   221, 223
Hamilton, Bryce   221, 223
Handy, Joe   ii, 149, 177
Harbin, Virginia   235-236
Harmon, Gail   223
Harnik, Peter   vii, 149, 178-179, 193, 223, 228, 235
Harris, John "Jay" IV   236
Harris, Michael   221
Hauge, Scott   156
Hayes, Denis   30, 179-181, 194, 222
Henderson, Hazel   iv, 149, 181-183, 235
Heritage, John   183
Herring, Dick   156
Hill, Gladwin   237

Hippocrates   107
Holman, M. Carl   237
honeybees   12, 87
Howe, Sydney   238-239
Huffington Post   7, 147
Hughes, Ted   24
humanism   59-60
Hunting, John   183-184, 236
Hutchings, Robert S.   239-240

I

Indian Ocean   9
indigenous people   222, 253
Issuu   157

J

Jackson, Wes   184-185
Jacobson, Michael F.   185-186
Jaskulski, Marcey   240
Jerabek, Sandra   223
jobs   vi, 19, 31, 83, 85, 86, 91, 115, 123, 127, 130, 157, 190
Johnson, Princess Daazhraii   253
Johnson, Ladybird   174-176, 232-233
Johnson, Samuel   111
Junior League   50

K

Keats, John   1
Kempf, Kyle   157
Kerley, Janet   156
Key, Vic   222
Kingsolver, Barbara   24
Kinane, Richard John   223
Kirchick, Jamie   73, 149, 152
Koralek, Craig   223
Krumboltz, Ann   223

L

Lampi, Ruth 223
Land and Water Conservation Fund Act 3
Lawson, Jerry 156
lead 2, 198
League of Women Voters 50, 180, 229
Lee, Charles 253
Lefkoff, Merle 186-187, 236
Lerza, Catherine 6-7, 150, 188-189, 193, 223
Levin, Yuval 79, 153
liberals 85, 100, 102, 122, 151-152, 155
Lilley, Robert 222
Love, Sam 150, 188-189, 222-223
Lovins, Amory iii, 150, 189-191
Lovins, L. Hunter 191
Lowery, Reverend Joseph 252
Luther, Martin 63-67
Lyman, Francesca 192-194, 223
Lynch, Chris 156

M

MacEachern, Diane 223
Malchon, Jeanne 240-241
Mark, Bill 222
Marshall, Sarah 150
Maslow, Abraham 43
Matthiessen, Peter 24
Mazzocchi, Anthony "Tony" 241
McCabe, W. Michael ix, 30, 150, 193, 194-195
McCarthy, Cormac 24
McCarthy, Gina 249
McCloskey, Peter 195, 216
McCracken, Todd 155
meat consumption 40-41, 140
meerkat 10
Meyer, Alden 223
Michael, Phil 223
Millennials 40, 47, 134, 143

Miller-Travis, Vernice 253
Mohai, Paul 253
Monbiot, George 113
Monroe, Marilyn 108
Montreal Protocol (1987) 2
Moore, April 223
Moore, Richard 253
Morgan, Rick 223
Mossett-White, Kandi 253
Moutray, Chad 156
movies 26
Moyer, Robin 222
Munoz, Irma 253
Munson, Dick 195-197, 223
museums 17, 25, 46

N

Nannis, Larry 156
National Geographic 8, 46
Native Americans 61, 104, 249, 252, 253
Neale, Henry 197-199
Nelson, Senator Gaylord 31, 179, 183, 246
Netflix 46
Netherlands 117
Nixon, President Richard 29
Norway 114

O

Ocean Dumping Ban Act 3, 12
Odell, W. Rice 242-243
organic change 4-5, 37, 76, 92-93, 101, 139, 151
Ottman, Jacquie 200-202
ozone layer 2, 193

P

Palmer, Chris 202-203
Parker, Carol 222, 223
Parque Patagonia 117

Parras, Juan   254
PBS *Nature* series   8, 10, 26, 46, 202
PCBs   2, 227
penguins   10
pesticides   2, 11, 12, 119, 185, 236, 252
Peterson, Gunnar A.   243
Pinder, Glenn David   148, 153, 225
Plumb, Tom   222
Pofeldt, Elaine   157
polarization   32-34, 43, 85, 93, 108
politics by other means   35-39, 104, 141-142
pollutants   2, 12
Pomerance, Rafe   203-204
pop music   25-26
Pope, Carl   73, 150, 204-205
population growth   13, 204, 236

R

Radin, Alex   243-244
Ramos, Lucy   254
Ramos, Norma   254
Rawson, Michael   viii, 148-149, 150, 205-206
Reagan, President Ronald   31, 173, 193, 195
recycling   18, 19, 196, 200, 210
Reilly, William K.   163, 206-207, 250
Renaissance   58-62, 138
renewable energy   15, 18-21, 82, 122, 124, 126-128, 166-167, 210-211, 213, 215, 216, 238
rewilding   5, 106, 111-121, 135, 138
Rewilding Europe   117
Rivera, Roger   254
Robinson, Gail   223
Roisman, Tony   223
Rooney, Angela   225, 244-245
Ryan, Hank   156

S

Safe Drinking Water Act   2, 248

Sagan, Carl 67
same-sex marriage 25, 36
Sandoval, Arturo 222
Satterthwaite, Ann 207-209
Schaeffer, Jan 222, 223
Schuck, Peter H. iii, 150, 152
Schumacher, E. F. xi, 154
The Science Channel 26
Scott, Doug 222, 223
Scruton, Sir Roger 153
self-organizing systems 5, 38, 87-89, 101, 106
Seydel, Scott Sr. 210
Shakespeare, William 107
Sheehan, Jack 245-246
Shelley, Percy 1
Silent Spring 11-12, 24, 241
The Simpsons 26
Sklar, Scott 15, 150, 210-211
small business vi, 19-20, 38, 86, 88-93, 146, 154-158
Small is Beautiful xi, 95, 146, 154
Smee, Sebastian 8, 42
Smith, James Noel 246
Speth, James Gustave "Gus" 211-213
Spurlock, Langley 150
Stansbery, Jeff 223
Stegner, Wallace 24
Sullivan, Thomas M. 156
The Sundance Channel 26
Sun Day 166, 180, 196, 213
Superfund program 2, 230
sustainability 55, 80, 91-92, 138, 139, 154, 165

T

Tafel, Rich v, 150, 153
Tarratt, Martin 150
Taylor, Jerry 153
Taylor, Patricia 223
television 25, 26, 36, 37, 42, 44, 46, 141
Thatcher, Margaret 24, 94-95

Thoreau, Henry David 42
Thunberg, Greta 6
toxic sites 2, 230
Tree, Isabella 118
trevally 9
Train, Russell E. 206, 247-248
Troutman, Mike 223
Trump, Donald 34, 43, 98, 101, 124, 128, 139
tuskfish 9

V

Van Wagenen, Lola 213

W

Walsh, Michaela 214-215
Wallick, Frank 222, 223
Wallick, Ruth 222, 223
Webb, Geoffrey 215-217
Weinberg, Ben 150
Welch, Kathleen 217
Wentworth, Marchant Lucky 222, 223
Werner, Carol & Jack 217-220
White, Reverend Leon 252
wilderness 3, 17, 110-111, 119, 174, 176, 227
Wilson, Professor E. O. 119-120
wolves 113-115, 202
Wright, Beverly L. 254

Y

Yeti crabs 8-9
Yeampierre, Elizabeth 254

Z

Zwick, David 248